Drug Cartel and Gang Violence in Mexico and Central America

A CONCISE INTRODUCTION

Newly Revised First Edition

Robert O. Kirkland

Union Institute & University

SAN DIEGO

Bassim Hamadeh, CEO and Publisher
Carrie Montoya, Manager, Revisions and Author Care
Kaela Martin, Project Editor
Jess Estrella, Senior Graphic Designer
Alexa Lucido, Licensing Manager
Natalie Piccotti, Director of Marketing
Kassie Graves, Vice President of Editorial
Jamie Giganti, Director of Academic Publishing

Printed in the United States of America.

CONTENTS

preface

The number of people killed in drug-related violence in Mexico and Central America over the past ten years has numbered in the tens of thousands. Most of the violence is rooted in the conflict between rival drug cartels for control of drug shipment routes.

Mexico's cartels control the majority of the drug trade from Colombia to the United States. Most cartels pay off local officials, extort businesses, and augment their bottom line through kidnappings for ransom. Mexico's security forces continue to battle against the drug cartels in an attempt to reestablish law and order.

Like Mexico, Central America has seen a rise in violence due to its importance as a transshipment point for cocaine to the United States. The drug trade in Central America is controlled by organized crime elements dominated by gangs. In many respects, these gangs are indistinguishable from the cartels that operate in Mexico.

The problem is serious. As a recent analyst with STRATFOR noted, the institutional weakness and security vulnerabilities of the Central American and Mexican states and the billions of dollars drugs command create what he called "an insurmountable challenge for the regional counternarcotic campaigns."

This purpose of this book is to give you a succinct overview of the issues and challenges associated with drugs, cartels, and gangs in Mexico and Central America today. Specifically, it will give you a compact but complete history of drug cartels in Mexico, lay out the current issues with drug enforcement and corruption in Mexico, detail the problem of increasing levels of violence and the rise of vigilantism in Mexico, and provide an overview of the issues associated with gangs and narcotrafficking in Central America.

Written by noted area specialists, each author has spent years analyzing the topics addressed through field research and interviews with regional leaders or local actors. The articles represent the most compact and up-to-date analysis of the issues involved.

It is my sincere hope that you will come away with a greater appreciation of the serious issues that Mexico and Central America face today in combating these "criminal insurgencies."

Dr. Robert Kirkland
Union Institute and University
Robertkirklandconsulting.com

one

The brutal cycle of violence known as Mexico's drug war has become one of the most destructive episodes in history linked to the narcotics trade. From 2006 to 2012, during which President Felipe Calderón waged a US-backed offensive against drug cartels, fighting between rival gangs and the security forces led to between 47,000 and 70,000 deaths. Mexican cartels have also expanded from drug trafficking to a portfolio of criminal activities, including kidnapping, extortion, oil theft, piracy, and human smuggling. However, drugs are still their main business and provide the glue that holds these organizations together. Drawing from 12 years of reporting on crime and narcotics in Mexico and extensive research for his book *El Narco: Inside Mexico's Criminal Insurgency*, Ioan Grillo examines how the cartels have grown within the context of a hundred years of US drug policy and how they continue to withstand the bilateral efforts to bring them down. In the second article, Duncan Breda and I evaluate the effectiveness of Operation Jalisco, a 2015–2018 Mexican government action to blunt the drug trafficking organization (DTO) Cartel Jalisco Nueva Generación (CJNG). Overall, we argue that Operation Jalisco has been ineffective against the CJNG in Jalisco. In the final article, Duncan Breda and I look at the cartel landscape in 2019, in particular examining the reform efforts of the new Mexican President, Andrés López Obrador.

MEXICAN CARTELS

A CENTURY OF DEFYING U.S. DRUG POLICY

By Ioan Grillo

The brutal cycle of violence known as Mexico's drug war has become one of the most destructive episodes in history linked to the narcotics trade. From 2006 to 2012, during which President Felipe Calderón waged a U.S.-backed offensive against drug cartels, fighting between rival gangs and the security forces led to between 47,000 and 70,000 deaths.[1] Even since President Enrique Peña Nieto took power in December 2012 and changed focus from security to the economy, thousands more have been murdered in cartel-related violence. Mexican cartels have also expanded from drug trafficking to a portfolio of criminal activities, including kidnapping, extortion, oil theft, piracy, and human smuggling. However, drugs are still their main business, and provide the glue that holds these organizations together. The deep roots of such organizations in many communities constitute one reason that Mexican cartels have been so resistant to the efforts against them. The Mexican-organized crime networks are a century

Ioan Grillo, "Mexican Cartels: A Century of Defying U.S. Drug Policy," The Brown Journal of World Affairs, vol. 20, no. 1, pp. 253–265. Copyright © 2013 by The Brown Journal of World Affairs. Reprinted with permission. Provided by ProQuest LLC. All rights reserved.

in the making, born at the beginning of the U.S. narcotics prohibition and expanding steadily through the decades of changing American drug use. Drawing from 12 years of reporting on crime and narcotics in Mexico and extensive research for my book, *El Narco*, this essay examines how the cartels have grown within the context of a hundred years of U.S. drug policy, and how they continue to withstand the bilateral efforts to bring them down.[2]

OPIUM SMUGGLERS

In the ramshackle village of Santiago de los Caballeros, on the slopes of the Sierra Madre Mountains in Mexico's Sinaloa state, residents call drug traffickers by the rather complimentary word *valientes*, or brave ones. The soldiers sent to fight traffickers, on the other hand, are referred to disdainfully as *gauchos*, an indigenous word for servants. Traffickers are also glorified in local ballads as heroes who beat the army and the Drug Enforcement Administration or as benevolent godfathers who shower villages with gifts. Such praise may contrast sharply with the reality of the cartels' masked death squads that are largely responsible for the pain and destruction. However, it comes from a drug trafficking culture that has developed over almost one hundred years and is deeply entrenched in these mountain communities.[3]

The Pacific state of Sinaloa is the cradle of Mexican organized crime, as Sicily is to the mafia. Sinaloans have grown opium poppies and smuggled their gum into the United States since the drug was first restricted under the Harrisons Narcotics Tax Act of 1914. The criminals of northwest Mexico were in an ideal position to take advantage of the first significant U.S. black market in drugs that resulted from the 1914 act. They were far from the center of power in Mexico City and close to a 2,000-mile border with the United States that has proven impossible to police. Sinaloa also boasted a large population of bandits and displaced peasants who were easily tempted by smuggling. Pink opium poppies had grown in this part of the Sierra

Madre since Chinese migrants came to build Sinaloa's railroads and toil in its mines in the late nineteenth century.

Mexico's first opium smugglers were the descendants of these migrants and early police records show convicts with Spanish Christian names and Chinese surnames—men such as Patricio Hong and Felipe Wong. One of the earliest U.S. investigations into this trade in 1916 reports how the Mexican and Chinese worked with Chinese opium syndicates in the United States in one case in San Francisco. That investigation also alleged that corrupt Mexican officials, including the then governor of Baja California, helped the smugglers.[4] This problem of corruption has frustrated efforts to curb the Mexican drug trade until the present day.

Mexican smuggling networks were boosted by another U.S. policy: the prohibition of alcohol. The "noble experiment" led to a surge in the cantinas in border cities catering to thirsty Americans while Mexican gangs also trafficked alcohol for illegal consumption in the United States. When prohibition was appealed in 1933, some moved over to the opium and heroin trade. One such bootlegger, Juan Nepomuceno, founded the criminal network that eventually became the Gulf Cartel.[5]

Mexican gangsters finally captured all of the country's opium trade from their Chinese counterparts amid a wave of racial violence in the 1930s. Rioters seized migrants and shifted them away in boxcars before expropriating their shops—or opium crops. A dispatch from the U.S. consul in Ensenada reported that organized crime figures were funding anti-migrant groups.[6] In other places, gangsters simply shot dead their rivals, such as in Ciudad Juárez, when a gunman working for a trafficker called La Nacha is reported to have murdered eleven Chinese men.[7] La Nacha, one of the first on a long list of female drug smugglers in Mexico, converted much of the Sinaloan opium into the more potent heroin, which was gaining popularity in the post-jazz age. She is reported to have sold it to many Texans, including soldiers from the base in El Paso and customers from as far as Albuquerque, New Mexico.[8]

Sinaloan opium production rose steadily in the 1940s. Many allege that the U.S. government directly aided this growth by purchasing opium to make morphine for its troops who were bleeding from German and

Japanese shells. The United States turned to Mexico, according to this theory, because German U-Boats disrupted the traditional supply of opium from Turkey.[9] Many of Sinaloa's present day politicians cite the existence of this deal and the idea of a pact written on the wall of Mexico's Defense Department in its history of the drug trade.[10] However, the director of the U.S. Federal Bureau of Narcotics at the time, the hardliner Harry Anslinger, vehemently denied any such pact.[11]

Whether or not they were helped by sales to the U.S. government, the opium profits provided a steady supply of income to mountain villages, such as Santiago, so that by the 1950s even a Sinaloa baseball team was known as the "gummers"—referring to those who made opium gum. Drug production was celebrated because it was seen as a route out of poverty and the trade became an integral part of the mountain culture—along with pickup trucks, folk saints, and Kalashnikov rifles. In this environment, many of today's most powerful cartel kingpins were raised, including Joaquin "Chapo" Guzman, born in 1957 in the village of La Tuna, up the mountain path from Santiago.

> MEXICAN SMUGGLING ACTIVITIES TRANSFORMED INTO NATIONAL NETWORKS DURING THE EXPLOSION OF U.S. DRUG CONSUMPTION IN THE 1960s AND 1970s.

FROM MARIJUANA TO COCAINE CARTELS

Mexican smuggling activities transformed into national networks during the explosion of U.S. drug consumption in the 1960s and 1970s. As the "hippie generation" smoked unprecedented amounts of marijuana, dealers went over the Rio Grande looking for the herb. Sinaloa could not meet the colossal demand, so farmers growing marijuana spread south along the Sierra Madre to states including Jalisco, Michoacán, Guerrero, and Oaxaca. Among the U.S. entrepreneurs seeking this marijuana was "Boston" George Jung, who was inspired by the movie *The Night of the Iguana* to fly down to Puerto Vallarta to score. He was soon making $100,000 a month flying the herbs up in light aircraft, before being arrested with a case full of marijuana at the Playboy club in Chicago. Jung later went on to become a major cocaine smuggler whose life story is featured in the movie *Blow*.[12]

In 1969, President Richard Nixon reacted to the northward tidal wave of drugs with Operation Intercept, in which agents searched every vehicle or pedestrian coming across the southern border while the army set up mobile radar units between posts. However, the operation wrecked havoc, backing up trucks of goods and preventing Mexican workers from traveling to their U.S. jobs. After a barrage of complaints, the government stopped Intercept after 17 days, evincing the grim reality that only selected vehicles could be checked. Today, the number of people and goods crossing the line has increased hundreds of times, reaching $500 billion of legal bilateral trade in 2012.

Mexico finally agreed to work with the United States on an aggressive anti-drug offensive known as Operation Condor from 1976 to 1978. The United States supplied Mexico with hardware—39 Bell Helicopters, 22 small aircrafts, and an executive jet—forming one of the largest police fleets in Latin America. Mexico sprayed crops up in the Sierra Madre, while soldiers stormed Sinaloan villages and arrested or shot dead many alleged traffickers.[13] The Mexican army was accused of widespread human rights abuses as it carried out the operation. A regional lawyers association said that 457 prisoners on drug charges in Sinaloa had suffered torture, including electric shocks,

> SELLING IN THE UNITED STATES FOR OVER ONE HUNDRED DOLLARS A GRAM, COCAINE TRANSFORMED LATIN AMERICAN SMUGGLERS FROM MILLIONAIRES TO BILLIONARIES.

burns, and rape. Despite these abuses, reports concur that Mexico's traffickers did suffer significant losses.[14]

The main drawback to Operation Condor was that many Sinaloan traffickers fled from the mountains to the urban sprawl of Guadalajara, establishing a major base of operations in Mexico's second largest city. Colombian marijuana growers, known by local historians as the Bonanza Marimbera, were also given a boost. These Colombian smuggling networks subsequently expanded into the even more profitable market of cocaine. Such movement is known in the drug war as the balloon effect—when you put pressure on one part of the balloon, the air simply moves to another part.

Selling in the United States for over one hundred dollars a gram, cocaine transformed Latin American smugglers from millionaires into billionaires. Amid the rise of the disco drug, people began to talk of cocaine cartels such as the Medellín Cartel in Colombia and their associates in Mexico's Guadalajara Cartel (made up of Sinaloans who had fled Condor). Some academics have criticized the use of the term, alleging that trafficking organizations are not really "cartels" because they do not attempt to fix prices. However, the word has survived for 30 years, used by law enforcement, journalists, and—importantly—the gangsters themselves, evidenced by names such as the Sinaloa Cartel and Gulf Cartel sprayed on walls to demarcate territory. The term "drug cartel," therefore, has thus assumed its own meaning.

The United States' attempts to combat the Guadalajara Cartel led to one of the darkest moments in U.S. drug work in Mexico: the 1985 murder of Drug Enforcement Administration (DEA) agent Enrique "Kiki" Camarena. The agent had helped raid enormous drug plantations linked to the cartel such as one in the Chihuahua desert that held thousands of tons of marijuana. Camarena also complained in his dispatches to Washington of a network of Mexican police protecting traffickers. As Camarena left the U.S. consulate in Guadalajara one day, five men abducted him. A month later, the agent's decomposing body was dumped on a road hundreds of miles away; he had suffered severe torture and had his skull smashed by a blunt object.[15]

Attacking the DEA was perhaps an overreach by the Guadalajara Cartel as, under U.S. pressure, its leaders were all arrested by 1989. However, the new generation of cartels that emerged in the 1990s proved only wealthier and more violent. The Mexican traffickers' wealth increased as they gradually took over most of the cocaine profits from their Colombian partners. U.S. law enforcement became highly effective at blocking the trafficking route from Colombia through the Caribbean Sea to Florida with a combination of naval ships and radars. Colombians thus shifted the vast majority of their product to Mexico where it could be trafficked over the 2,000-mile border. By 2010, the DEA estimated that 93 percent of cocaine entering the United States passed through Mexico. It was another example of the drug war's balloon effect. Mexicans began as paid couriers, but they gradually took over ownership of the cocaine and its wholesale in the United States. Jay Bergman, the DEA's Andean Director, describes how the Mexican domination over the Colombians took place largely without bloodshed:

> What is interesting is that there was no hostile takeover or violence. At each progression, the Colombian cartels made a conscious decision to allocate more share to the Mexicans ... Who really calls the shots in a global supply and demand economy? Is it Mexican cartels or Colombian cocaine suppliers? Is it the manufacturer or the distributor? In a legitimate economic model, is it Colgate or Walmart that calls the shots? It is actually Walmart who says, 'This is what we want to pay for it, this is a unit price, this is when we want it delivered, and this is how its going to be' ... That is the evolved cocaine market we are dealing with.[16]

Mexico's billionaire cartels also appeared to penetrate increasingly higher levels of the political establishment. Some of the most high profile accusations were leveled at Raul Salinas, brother of President Carlos Salinas, who served from 1988 to 1994. In 1995, Swiss authorities found $110 million in accounts linked to Raul Salinas and began money laundering proceedings against him, with Swiss detectives alleging the funds were linked to drug traffickers. In 2008, Switzerland gave $77 million from the accounts to the Mexican government on the grounds that it had criminal origins.[17] Raul Salinas has denied links to traffickers. He was arrested in Mexico in 1995 for masterminding a murder and served ten years in prison before being acquitted. In July 2013, a Mexican court cleared him of illicit enrichment, although federal prosecutors said they would appeal the decision. In another high profile case in 1997, Mexico's own drug czar Jose de Jesus Gutierrez Rebollo, whose story is fictionalized in the drug smuggling movie *Traffic*, was arrested and convicted of working with cartels.[18]

"THE MEXICAN DRUG WAR"

Almost no one predicted the level of violence that Mexican cartels would unleash in the twenty-first century. In 2000, the news media was focused less on crime and more on how President Vicente Fox had unseated the Institutional Revolutionary Party (PRI) after 71 years in power. Another major story dwelt on the Zapatista rebels and their post-modernist leader Subcomandate Marcos, who smoked a pipe and recited poetry. However, the number of cartel-related murders increased steadily under Fox, from 1,304 in 2004 to over 2,100 in 2006, according to government figures.[19] When President Felipe Calderón took power in December that year and launched a national offensive against traffickers, related homicides rocketed, reaching 15,272 in 2010.[20]

Various factors can be considered to explain the explosion of violence. One is the cumulative effect of pumping so much money into cartels. There is extensive disagreement over how much Mexican traffickers make smuggling drugs into the United States since no one is privy to cartel balance sheets; estimates range from some $6 billion to $40 billion a year.[21] But either way, over a 20-year period the sum is likely to reach hundreds of billions of dollars. That money bought a rising pile of guns, corrupt police, and paid assassins, who increasingly turned on each other.

Another factor that might have incited violence could be the repeal of the assault weapons ban in the United States in 2004, the same year that violence in Mexico began to increase significantly. Between 2007 and 2011, Mexican security forces captured 99,000 guns and the U.S. Bureau of Alcohol, Tobacco, Firearms and Explosives (ATF) traced 68,000 of them—more than two-thirds—to U.S. gun sellers.[22] Most were automatic rifles, including Kalashnikovs and AR-15s. However, cartel gunmen have also been found with heavy weaponry, including fragmentation grenades and RPG-7 rocket launchers, stolen from Central American armed forces.

> ALMOST NO ONE PREDICTED THE LEVEL OF VIOLENCE THAT MEXICAN CARTELS WOULD UNLEASH IN THE TWENTY-FIRST CENTURY.

A key element in the violence was certainly the change of power from the one-party rule of the PRI to a multiparty system. From 2000 to 2012, the center-right National Action Party (PAN) held the presidency but had a minority in both houses of Congress and among state governors and mayors. The PRI, the center-left Democratic Revolution Party, and another four smaller parties held the rest of the posts.

The PAN presidents Fox and Calderón claim that, unlike the PRI, they went after drug cartels, which inadvertently created more violence. But critics also point to a fragmentation of security forces under multiparty rule. Whereas under the twentieth-century PRI, almost all police and soldiers answered to authorities in the same political party, democratic rule saw competing political groups control different municipal, state, and federal forces. In some cases, different police forces controlled by different political groups actively fought each other. For example, in 2009, state police in Michoacán are alleged to have taken part in attacks on federal police that killed 15 officers.

Another problem was that increasing numbers of soldiers, marines, and police officers defected to join the ranks of cartels. The most notorious case was that of the Zetas, founded in the late 1990s by 14 former soldiers as enforcers for the Gulf Cartel. The Zetas went on to recruit many of the former comrades as well as police officers and gang members who they trained to become an ultra-violent paramilitary force in the new millennium. They finally turned on their former masters in the Gulf Cartel in 2010, and became one of the most powerful and blood thirsty criminal organizations in the hemisphere. Their militarization of the conflict was soon followed by other cartels, who also recruited former soldiers and used paramilitary tactics.

Calderón's offensive against cartels only exacerbated the violence. While Calderón launched his campaign without immediate pressure from the United States, Washington was quick to praise and underwrite it with some $300 million a year in training and hardware under the Mérida initiative. U.S. law enforcement agencies also supported the offensive with increasingly aggressive stings on cartels often involving paid informants and infiltrators. Such intelligence led to the arrest or shooting of several major cartel kingpins, including Arturo Beltrán Leyva, "The Beard," whom Mexican marines shot dead in 2009. Other U.S. operations came under severe criticism, such as the so-called "Fast and Furious." In that sting, ATF agents allowed certain weapons bought in U.S. gun shops to cross the border, with the hope of bringing down the entire guns network. This backfired, however, as the weapons ultimately ended up in the possession of murderous cartels.[23]

> CALDERÓN'S OFFENSIVE AGAINST CARTELS ONLY EXACERBATED THE VIOLENCE. WHILE CALDERÓN LAUNCHED HIS CAMPAIGN WITHOUT IMMEDIATE PRESSURE FROM THE UNITED STATES, WASHINGTON WAS QUICK TO PRAISE AND UNDERWRITE IT.

While some Mexican soldiers were involved in the fight against drug traffickers since at least the 1960s, Calderón brought the military involvement to new levels. By 2011, there were 96,000 soldiers and 16,000 Mexican marines in the campaign against cartels. The offensive focused on bringing down the kingpins—a technique known as decapitating the cartel, or removing its head. The Mexican government compiled a list of 37 key traffickers, and 25 were arrested or shot dead by the time Calderón left office. Security forces also made record busts, including 23 tons of cocaine from a ship in the port of Manzanillo and $207 million in cash from a mansion in Mexico City.[24]

But whenever a kingpin was taken down it appeared to provoke more violence as their lieutenants or rivals fought over their territory. For example, following the killing of Beltrán Leyva in December 2009, the number of homicides in the state spiked, from 259 in 2009 to 487 in 2010.[25] Furthermore, the new cartel leaders replacing the fallen were increasingly violent, carrying out massacres and mass beheadings on a horrific scale. One was Óscar Osvaldo Garcia, a former marine, who had worked as a hit man for Beltán Leyva but went on to command his own bloodthirsty criminal group. When the police arrested him in 2011, he said he had personally carried out 300 murders and ordered another 300.[26]

The gun battles between security forces and cartel gunmen also terrified citizens, rather than making them feel safer. Residents, workers, and school children often cowered from firefights that could last hours in broad daylight. Worse, the security forces killed dozens of civilians who failed to stop at checkpoints or were in the line of fire. Soldiers were also accused of widespread human rights abuses, including torture, rape, and murder of those they detained.

Finally, despite its high human cost, the offensive did not have any conclusive impact on drug trafficking itself. The total amount of drugs seized on the U.S. southern border actually went up during Calderón's administration. In 2010, U.S. agents seized 4.5 tons of crystal meth, 905 kilos of heroin, 1,500 tons of marijuana, and 17.8 tons of cocaine coming from Mexico. This was comparable to 2.7 tons of meth, 449 kilos of heroin,

1,046 tons of marijuana, and 27 tons of cocaine in 2006.[27] The change may have been because U.S. agents had become better at finding drugs due to more officers—or more drugs could be heading north. Interestingly, the only drug to show a reduction in seizures was cocaine, while the amount of crystal meth increased the most—a fact that may reflect changing drug preferences among American users.

Ultimately, Calderón's offensive against cartels will be judged by history as a failure. He neither significantly impacted their ability to traffic drugs nor increased the sense of security among most Mexicans. The total homicide rate shot up from about 8,800 in 2007, his first full year in office, to more than 26,000 in his last in 2012.[28] A core drawback was certainly the fragmentation of state security forces as discussed. But Calderón also faced the insurmountable logic of fighting the drug trade: as long as there are multibillion dollar profits in trafficking drugs, there will be criminals to take the place of those killed or arrested. And in an ultra-violent criminal environment such as Mexico, the most aggressive ruthless traffickers become the most dominant, with each generation proving more bloodthirsty than the last.

CHANGING THE CONVERSATION

When Peña Nieto took office in December 2012, returning the PRI to presidential power after 12 years in the wilderness, he said he would change the security priority from attacking traffickers to reducing the homicide rate. "I reaffirm the Mexican state's obligation to combating drug trafficking," Peña Nieto said in an interview with news agency *Reuters*. "But now we have another matter which for me takes higher priority, that of the violence."[29] His goal, he said, was to halve the homicide rate during his six years in office.[30]

Reducing the number of murders could be a tough battle. There were about 6,000 cartel-related homicides in the first six months of Peña Nieto's presidency, according to the government's figures.[31] The administration assures this is a reduction of 16 percent, compared to the same period a year before, but others have questioned whether fewer homicides are being classified as cartel murders. It has also proved difficult to return soldiers to their barracks because of the complicated security situation. Following fighting between cartels and a new wave of citizen vigilante militias in the state of Michoacán, Peña Nieto sent military units there to restore the peace in May 2013.

Violence also rages in the northeast of Mexico and in Sinaloa state. The Sinaloa Cartel continues as the wealthiest trafficking organization in Mexico, making billions selling cocaine, heroin, marijuana, and crystal meth.[32] Almost a century after Sinaloans first began smuggling opium into the United States, their profits from the drug trade are as lucrative as ever.

But whatever the real changes on the ground, the Peña Nieto government has been very effective in changing the agenda in the media. The practice of parading suspected traffickers in front of reporters has been abandoned and officials have switched from talking about security to focusing on the economy. When President Barack Obama visited Mexico in May 2013, the two presidents focused on trade and immigration rather than drugs. Mexico also announced it was reorganizing the cooperation between U.S. law enforcement agencies and their Mexican counterparts, so they would go through official channels rather than agents dealing directly with each other. Obama raised no objections to the new position. "It is obviously up to the Mexican people to determine their security structures and how it engages with other nations—including the United States," he said.[33] Following the level of violence during Calderón's term, neither Mexico City nor Washington appeared to have much appetite for a renewed offensive on the cartels.

Diverting the conversation from drug trafficking and related violence is a legitimate strategy. It is understandable that the Mexican government does not want to let thousands of criminals dominate the national agenda in a country of 115 million. There is also little to be gained by the United States trying to pressure for stronger action against drug trafficking in Mexico given the experience of the last six years. However, the Mexican and U.S. governments still need to get to the root causes of the problem to stem the violence and power of cartels in the long term. In Mexico, this means following through on efforts to build a functioning justice system that can turn around terrible rates of impunity. A historic justice reform approved in 2008 rules that Mexico changes from a closed door, written trial system to an open oral system by 2016. All support from U.S. institutions in this Herculean task will be extremely useful. The Peña Nieto government has also launched a national crime prevention program to try and stop the next generation of young men from becoming traffickers and assassins. The scheme supports the work of many independent social workers who have been laboring for years in the most vulnerable communities trying to steer people away from crime. International funding for such social work projects is also money well spent. The Peña Nieto government may also have some success with proposals to unify municipal, state, and federal forces under single commands. This process began in Michoacan in August 2013, where the government put all police and soldiers under a unified leadership to counter the wanton violence in the state. If a root of Mexico's recent cartel problem was a fragmentation of the state apparatus as discussed in the previous section, than a unifying of forces could be a key part of the solution.

IN THE UNITED STATES, THE SOLUTION COULD ALSO MEAN A RADICAL RETHINK OF DRUG POLICY TO STOP BILLIONS MORE DOLLARS OF DRUG MONEY FROM FALLING INTO THE HANDS OF CARTELS.

In the United States, the solution could also mean a radical rethinking of drug policy to stop billions more dollars of drug money from falling into the hands of cartels and paying for more guns, hit men, and corruption in the decades to come. Drug policy reform, which may mean the legalization of soft drugs such as marijuana and more focus on treatment rather than punishment of users of harder drugs such as heroin, will not make Mexico's cartels completely disappear. As described earlier, they have also diversified to other heinous criminal activities from extortion to kidnapping. But U.S. drug policy reform could weaken cartels decisively so they will no longer overwhelm Mexican security forces. Instead of being a national security problem for Mexico like they are today, they could become a criminal problem, as the mafia and such groups are in the United States.

CONCLUSION

For over a century, Mexican traffickers have made countless billions of dollars from the U.S. black market in drugs. During this time, they have survived the long list of attempts to destroy them by U.S. agencies—from operations on the border to crop spraying to the arrest of dozens of king-pins. The Mexican cartels have also adapted to an array of different Mexican governments, at times fleeing to other parts of the country, bribing high-level officials, or employing extreme violence. The most important offensive against the cartels, from 2006 to 2012, failed to have a significant impact on the drug trade. Mexico City and Washington currently appear resigned to limiting the damage of the cartels, arresting some traffickers, and seizing some drugs, rather than keen on making a serious effort to end the cross-border trade in narcotics.

NOTES

1. International Crisis Group, *Peña Nieto's Challenge: Criminal Cartels and the Rule of Law in Mexico* (March 19, 2013), 2, 47. This report details the different counts of cartel-related homicides in Mexico by Mexico's federal attorney general's office and media organizations.

2. Ioan Grillo, *El Narco: Inside Mexico's Criminal Insurgency* (New York: Bloomsbury, 2011).

3. Grillo, *El Narco*, 17–37.

4. Luis Astorga, *Drogas Sin Fronteras: Los Expedientes de una Guerra Permanente* (Mexico City: Grijalbo, 2003), 17.

5. Cesar Peralta Gonzalez, "Fallecio el fundador del cartel del Golfo," *El Universal*, July 12, 2001.

6. Grillo, *El Narco*, 32; Astorga, *Drogas Sin Fronteras*.

7. Jose Luis Garcia Cabrera, *1920–2000, El Pastel! Parte Dos* (Mexico City: Palibrio, 2012), 102.

8. "Todavia No Han Logrado Aprehender a 'La Nacha,'" *El Continental*, August 22, 1933.

9. Manuel Lazcano, *Vida en la Vida Sinoaloaense*, ed. Nery Cordova (Culiacan Mexico, 1992), 202.

10. Grillo, *El Narco*, 35–36.

11. Astorga, *Drogas Sin Fronteras*, 138–39.

12. Bruce Porter, *BLOW: How a Small-Town Boy Made $100 Million with the Medellin Cocaine Cartel and Lost It All* (New York: St Martins Griffin, 2001).

13. Elaine Shannon, *Desperados: Latin Drug Lords, U.S. Lawmen and the War America Can't Win* (New York: Viking, 1988), 62–69.

14. Ibid, 67.

15. Ibid, 222–30.

16. Grillo, *El Narco*, 82, 138.

17. "Salinas funds finally head back to Mexico," *SwissInfo*, June 18, 2008.

18. The arrest of Gutierrez Rebollo is cited by Mexico's Federal Attorney General's Office, Procurador General de La Republica, in Boletin, No. 27/0/97.

19. "Ejecuciones en México equivalen a un tercio de muertes en Irak desde 2003," *El Universal*, June 5, 2007.

20. International Crisis Group, *Peña Nieto's Challenge*, 47.

21. A vast range of estimates of the amount that Mexican cartels earn have been made by prosecutors, police officers, think tanks, and journalists on both sides of the border. In *El Narco*, 133–51, I analyze in more detail the economics of the drug trade. For one of the lower end estimates, see: Alejandro Hope and Eduard

Clark, "Si Los Vecinos Legalizan—Repore Tecnico," *IMCO* (October 2012), 45. For higher end estimates, see: "National Drug Threat Assessment 2009," National Drug Intelligence Center, U.S. Justice Department (December 2008); and Anna Mulrine, "Pentagon: Central America 'deadliest' non-war zone in the world," *Christian Science Monitor*, April 12, 2011.

22. For ATF numbers in press statement, see: "ATF Releases Government of Mexico Firearms Trace Data," ATF, April 26, 2012.

23. Committee on Oversight and Government Reform, U.S. House of Representatives, *Issa, Grassley Report on Fast & Furious Finds Widespread Justice Department Management Failures* (October 2012).

24. Grillo, *El Narco,* 115, 150–51.

25. Homicide rates as recorded by Mexico's National Institute of Statistic and Geography (INEGI).

26. Garcia gave a videotaped testimony to state prosecutors. For sections of this video, see: "Declaraciones de El Compayito El lider de La Mano con Ojos," *YouTube*, August 16, 2011.

27. National Drug Intelligence Center, U.S. Justice Department, *National Drug Threat Assessment* (2011).

28. Total homicide count by the Mexican government's national statistics agency INEGI. Also Professor James Creechan of the University of Guelph, Canada has done valuable work mining through INEGI data.

29. Anahi Rama and Dave Graham, "Mexico's Peña Nieto plans new police to fight drug gangs," *Reuters*, April 9, 2012.

30. "Busca Pena bajar 50% homicidios," *Reforma*, October 13, 2012.

31. "Presume Peña menos de mil ejecuciones en mayo; van 6 mil 250 en su sexeni," *Proceso*, June 6, 2013.

32. Patrick Radden Keefe, "Cocaine Incorporated," *New York Times*, June 15, 2012.

33. Mark Felsenthal and Steve Holland, "Obama blesses Mexican security plan, eyes deeper business ties," *Reuters*, May 3, 2013.

OPERATION JALISCO

EVALUATION OF MEXICO'S RESPONSE TO THE CJNG IN THE MEXICAN STATE
OF JALISCO—2015–2018

By Robert Kirkland and Duncan Breda

INTRODUCTION

The purpose of the article is to briefly evaluate the effectiveness of Operation Jalisco, a 2015–2018 Mexican government action to blunt the drug trafficking organization (DTO) Cartel Jalisco Nueva Generación (CJNG). Overall, we will argue that Operation Jalisco has been ineffective against the CJNG in Jalisco. Immigration lawyers can use the information in this article to bolster arguments that clients who fear the CJNG if returned to Jalisco continue to have valid concerns despite pronouncements from the Mexican government otherwise.

THE CJNG AND JALISCO

The CJNG is probably the most powerful cartel in Mexico and has expanded their territory across Mexico exponentially since 2015. The US Treasury Department has labeled the CJNG "one of the world's most prolific and violent drug trafficking organizations," and the Mexican government considers the CJNG the most powerful cartel in Mexico. CJNG's leader, Nemesio "El Mencho" Oseguera Cervantes, is the most wanted man in Mexico and is the number one high-value target for the Mexican intelligence services.

Jalisco is a crucial state to control for any Mexican DTO. Jalisco's climate and varying elevations allow for prime conditions for the production of opium poppies and marijuana plants. In addition, the ports of Puerto Vallarta and Manzanillo provide access to imported chemicals for DTOs' core profit maker, methamphetamine. The CJNG considers control of Jalisco as central to its operations.

OPERATION JALISCO

Starting in May 2015, the Mexican government commenced Operation Jalisco with the objectives of "capturing members of criminal groups [prominently the CJNG] and holding them accountable before the law ... [and to] cut off sources of income and capture its leaders." In the last three years, the operation has resulted in the capture of 13 ranked members of the CJNG, culminating in May 2018 with the arrest of El Mencho's wife, Rosalinda Gonzalez Valencia.

Despite these high-profile captures, Operation Jalisco has had more setbacks than successes. In the last three years, the toll has included an army Cougar helicopter shot down by a rocket-propelled grenade, killing eight soldiers, and the destruction of scores of banks and businesses. Recently, following the capture of El Mencho's wife, the CJNG stormed a restaurant, targeting former Jalisco state prosecutor Luis Carlos Nájera, injuring several patrons and killing an eight-month-old baby.

Nevertheless, Operation Jalisco has been deemed a success by government officials due to the capture of key leaders and financiers. Mexican government figures, however, prove otherwise. Drug trafficking in Jalisco grew 40 percent from 2015 to 2017. Violence was also up in 2018, with 415 murders committed during the first three months of the year, which is equivalent to 57 percent of the total murders in 2015. The CJNG continues to expand its power, with El Mencho operating with near impunity.

According to experts, Operation Jalisco's government-led kinetic operations cannot continue to be the backbone of stopping Mexican DTOs. These operations have only contributed to increasing cycles of violence over the past decade. The goal, according to experts, should be *conflict transformation* through a multiagency governmental approach that will restore the local citizenry's trust in the government to provide safety, security, and the freedom to live and work without fearing both the government and the DTOs. However, there is no indication so far that Mexico is moving in this direction.

CONCLUSION

Operation Jalisco has not achieved the results hoped for by the Mexican government. Drug trafficking and violence has increased since the operation, and the CJNG has expanded its power and influence in the last three years. Deportees who return to Jalisco will face an ever more violent state—one even more fraught with danger than the one they fled before 2019.

MEXICAN DRUG CARTELS IN 2019

By Robert Kirkland and Duncan Breda

Mexican drug cartels experienced a shakeup of power in 2016 that will have lasting effects for the foreseeable future. The traditional large drug cartels have had their control diminished. This has led to the fragmentation of the cartels throughout much of Mexico—a process known as balkanization.

Mexico has been very proactive over the last five years in its efforts to combat drug cartels. Troops as well as federal police have been deployed throughout the country. The capture (and recent conviction) of Sinaloa cartel leader Joaquin "El Chapo" Guzman Loera is the most recent success in a long line of drug cartel kingpins who have been killed or captured by Mexican authorities.

Right now in Mexico, areas of cartel influence can be broken down into three distinct geographical areas:

Sinaloa—Sinaloa Federation, Beltran Leyva Organization, Los Mazatlecos, and El Chapo Trini/El Cadete

Tierra Caliente (Mexican States of Michoacán, Guerrero, and the Federal District)—Cartel de Jalisco Nueva Generación, Knights Templar, and La Familia Michoacana

Tamaulipas—Los Zetas factions, Gulf Cartel, and the Velazquez network

With the increased fragmentation of cartels and the relinquishing of control by major cartels, smaller cartel groups have gained significant power—specifically, the Jalisco New Generation Cartel (CJNG) in the Tierra Caliente region. The most prominent example of the cartel's power came in May 2016 when the CJNG shot down a Mexican army helicopter. The CNJG has expanded their territory into areas controlled by the Sinaloa and Los Zetas Cartels. Despite some key losses of leaders in the CJNG in 2018, they continued to show that they were a force to be taken seriously by the Mexican authorities.

Tijuana saw a major increase in violence in 2018, with the CJNG battling the previously dominant Sinaloa Cartel for control of this important gateway to the US. In the past, the Sinaloa Cartel has used the softer tactics of corruption and persuasion to win control of areas, whereas the CJNG has more often turned to violence and their paramilitaries to seize power. The use of paramilitaries so close to the border has caused the US Treasury Department to label the CJNG "one of the world's most prolific and violent drug trafficking organizations."

The cartels' focus on the type of drugs they transport to the US changed in 2018 and will continue well into 2019. Mexican drug cartels have started to manufacture more designer drugs, specifically fentanyl. This is the same drug that infamously killed the music icon Prince in 2016. The drug has seen a rapid increase in popularity in the US. Due to the increase in demand, cartels have constructed labs in which they can easily produce the drug all in the same place. Fentanyl is up to forty times more potent that heroin. The increased potency causes a much higher dependency in the user, which in turn leads to an increased demand for the drug. Being able to produce the drug solely in a laboratory has also increased the cartels' profit margin. Cartels no longer need to buy the ingredients necessary to produce drugs from their South American counterparts. The demand for opiates and pharmaceuticals within the United States has increased the cartels' production of this dangerous drug and resulted in the DEA recently warning that there would be a drastic increase in the availability of these drugs in 2019.

Inside Mexico, the cartels have also moved into fuel theft. The equipment needed to tap into a fuel line is extremely inexpensive. Cartels can easily steal the fuel from these lines and then sell it for much less than the Mexican petroleum monopoly Pemex (Petróleos Mexicanos). When one adds the cartels' fuel profits to those they receive from illegal drugs, the profits often exceed the budgets of the Mexican states in which they operate.

In 2018, the Mexican people elected Andrés López Obrador to their six-year presidency. "Peace and reconciliation to our country" are two general goals of López Obrador and his new head of public security, Alfonso Durazo. They believe cartels can be diminished by granting amnesty to those not involved in human rights abuses, such as kidnapping, torture, and murder. In effect, lower-level cartel members would be pried away from their bosses. In addition, the new administration plans to move to a strong emphasis on countering money laundering and corruption and increasing the salaries and training of local police. The hope here is that with the amnesty in particular, cartels can be brought under control.

One might draw comparisons between López Obrador's approach and the amnesty program put in place by El Salvador's president, Mauricio Funes, in 2012. By the end of 2011, Funes concluded the heavy-handed nature of dealing with gangs such as MS-13 and M18 needed to be changed. In March 2012, he brokered a truce between the gangs and the government and granted wide-ranging concessions, which included withdrawing police and army troops from gang-controlled areas.

In evaluating the effectiveness of the truce, analysts noted that the gangs became stronger, given the decreased pressure from the government. One of the major shifts was that the gangs became aware of the potential to exercise real political influence based on territorial control, armed power, and access to increasing resources. In addition, the gangs, given the reprieve, consolidated their ties with Mexican drug cartels from a position of increasing strength.

Mauricio Funes's successor, Salvador Sánchez Cerén, realized that the truce was not working and declared war on the gangs again in 2016. This resulted in open warfare, and El Salvador once again became one of the most violent countries outside a recognized war zone, although the monthly average of some 440 homicides was not far below the monthly average of 521 victims during the country's civil war.

Clearly, López Obrador cannot go back to the "blind-eye" pre-2006 approach. When the Colombians were forced to find other routes to market cocaine in the 2000s, the Mexican transnational criminal organizations began to dominate the lucrative drug trade and grew in power. A 2019 amnesty or a truce will likely make the cartels stronger by giving them breathing space to regroup and consolidate their power in much the same way M18 and MS-13 did in El Salvador. The Mexican cartels have been curiously silent in reacting to López Obrador's proposals. It is likely that they see the amnesty offer as advantageous—giving them a reprieve from the continual pressure on their operations from the Mexican government over the last 12 years. Any such move in their mind is good policy.

In summary, 2018 saw a major shakeup in the cartel lands with a fragmentation of cartels and the rise of the CJNG. The decrease of marijuana trafficking and the increase of heroin, methamphetamine, and fentanyl production will continue well into 2019. 2019 will continue to be a violent year, with a continued battle among the cartels as they seek to consolidate their control of the drug trade. The cartel landscape is constantly changing, and 2019 will be no different despite the election of Andrés López Obrador.

two

C orruption plays a central role in the drug trafficking and the related "war" that have violently scarred Mexico in recent years. Corruption facilitates the operation of Mexico's vast and powerful criminal-business enterprises while simultaneously debilitating the state's efforts to confront them. But corruption and the structural weaknesses characterizing Mexico's institutions of justice are hardly new. This reading by Professor Stephen Morris of Middle Tennessee State first draws on recent events to describe the role of corruption in facilitating drug trafficking and handicapping the state, and then explores the underlying changes that have altered the historical and once-stable pattern. Mexico suffers a glaring "rule of law deficit." State institutions lack the capacity to enforce the law vis-à-vis society or themselves. But recent experience shows that launching a war against powerful drug traffickers and criminal organizations without the capacity to adequately do so leaves the state with few tools but force itself, resulting in a spiral of violence and an unprecedented level of insecurity.

CORRUPTION, DRUG TRAFFICKING, AND VIOLENCE IN MEXICO

By Stephen D. Morris

C orruption plays a central role in the drug trafficking and the related "war" that have violently scarred Mexico in recent years. Corruption facilitates the operation of Mexico's vast and powerful criminal-business enterprises while simultaneously debilitating the state's efforts to confront them. In fact, corruption makes it difficult at times to differentiate violators from enforcers. As poet, social activist, and grieving father of one victim of the war on drugs Javier Sicilia laments, "I don't know where the state ends and organized crime begins."[1] But corruption and the structural weaknesses characterizing Mexico's institutions of justice are hardly new. Corruption has long shaped Mexican politics and the

Stephen D. Morris, "Corruption, Drug Trafficking, and Violence in Mexico," The Brown Journal of World Affairs, vol. 18, no. 2, pp. 29-43. Copyright © 2012 by The Brown Journal of World Affairs. Reprinted with permission. Provided by ProQuest LLC. All rights reserved.

drug trade, yet never have these factors conspired to generate the degree of violence, brutality, and instability seen in recent years. This historical paradox—wherein drug-related corruption once contributed to or at least coexisted with low levels of violence and relative stability but now fuels the opposite—raises questions about the shifting patterns of corruption, the threads that tie it to drug trafficking and violence, and the dynamics unleashed by Mexican President Felipe Calderón's "war of choice" on organized crime. This brief essay first draws on recent events to describe the role of corruption in facilitating drug trafficking and handicapping the state, and then explores the underlying changes that have altered the historical and once-stable pattern.

CORRUPTION AND DRUG TRAFFICKING

Most scholars, public officials, and members of the general public agree that organizations providing contraband goods and services (i.e., organized crime including drug trafficking organizations) *cannot* operate without corruption: that the two—corruption and organized crime—are inherently linked, pointing to a type of corrupt bargain.[2] Studies of early twentieth-century prohibition in the United States and the operation of gambling and prostitution rings in major cities throughout the country today, for instance, both highlight the role illegal payoffs to police and local officials play not only in allowing these businesses to operate, but also in maintaining their activities and influence within certain geographic and political bounds.[3] With respect to Mexico, most experts agree on this point. As Laurie Freeman, a former associate of the Washington Office on Latin America, notes, "Doing business [in Mexico] entails bribing and intimidating public officials and law enforcement and judicial agents [...] organized crime cannot survive without corruption."[4] During a 2008 meeting of the *Consejo Nacional de Seguridad Pública* (National Council of Public Security), President Felipe Calderón (2006–2012) echoed this sentiment:

"The insecurity and violence that the country is living through is the result of [...] corruption that has become a cancer."[5]

The evidence of a corrupt bargain wherein corrupt state officials support and sustain drug trafficking in Mexico is overwhelming. Headlines periodically feature the arrest or detention of top officials within agencies spearheading the fight against drugs and organized crime (a federal responsibility); port and prison officials; military and police commanders; governors and gubernatorial candidates; state police, investigators, and district attorneys; mayors and city officials; and hundreds of municipal police, all for essentially aiding and abetting organized crime. For example, in November 2008, during the high profile *Operación Limpieza* (Operation Clean House), six members of SIEDO (*Subprocuraduría de Investigación Especializada en Delincuencia Organizada)*, the attorney general's office in charge of investigating and prosecuting organized crime, the head of the Mexican office of Interpol, directors of the federal police, and close associates of the secretary of public security were arrested for their ties to the Beltrán Leyva cartel.[6] Noé Ramírez, the former director of SIEDO, reportedly received $450,000 per month for his services to the cartel's leaders.[7]

This was not the first time that key officials in charge of fighting drug trafficking and organized crime had been discovered to be in the pay of drug traffickers. In 1997, General José Gutiérrez Rebollo, then head of the *Instituto Nacional para el Combate a las Drogas* (National Anti-Drug Institute) was arrested for his ties to *el Señor de los Cielos,* Amado Carillo Arrellano, the leader of the Juárez cartel. In May 2009, the federal government raided the western state of Michoacán, arresting a total of 38 public officials, including the former director of public security, the former state attorney general, and various mayors for their support of La Familia cartel.[8] All were eventually freed, however, for lack of evidence. In May 2010 in the state of Quintana Roo—just weeks after

CRIMINAL ORGANIZATIONS WERE REPORTEDLY SPENDING MORE THAN $500 MILLION A YEAR IN BRIBES.

former governor Mario Villanueva was extradited to the United States on charges of receiving $19 million from the Juárez cartel—the gubernatorial candidate and former mayor of Cancún Gregorio Sánchez was detained for alleged ties to the Beltrán Leyva and Zetas criminal organizations. In late January 2012, reports surfaced that the government was investigating three recent governors of the border state of Tamaulipas for possible ties to the Gulf cartel.[9]

Though evidence suggests that corruption and collusion reach into the highest and lowest layers of the Mexican government, the municipality constitutes the social base of organized crime. This is the place, as Kenny and Serrano note, "where Mexican policemen became criminals."[10] The newspaper *Reforma* reports that, of the 357 Mexican law enforcement officials detained in 2009 for assisting narco-traffickers, 90 percent belonged to local police forces.[11] Indeed, a study by the National Conference of Secretaries of Public Security estimated that 93.6 percent of municipal police depend on corruption to supplement their low salaries.[12] This historic pattern is incredibly sticky and seemingly immune from periodic and ritualistic purges, as well as purification and professionalization efforts.[13] Thousands of officials and police officers have been dismissed over the years because of corruption, and entire departments and agencies have been disbanded. Yet, as Charles Bowden notes, "In over a half century of fighting drugs, Mexico has never created a police unit that did not join the traffickers."[14]

By the 1990s, criminal organizations were reportedly spending more than $500 million a year in bribes—double the budget of the Attorney General's office (the *Procuraduría General de la República*, or PGR).[15] According to Héctor de Mauleón, author of *Atentamente, El Chapo* (Sincerely, El Chapo), "every trafficker has a great many appointed officials and elected politicians on his payroll."[16] Clearly, these extralegal payments are designed to neutralize the state's enforcement of laws against the illicit activities of the cartels. Thus, payoffs target those directly responsible for state enforcement efforts, including preventive and investigative police at both the federal and state levels, the municipal police at the local level, military commanders, *ministerios publicos* (officials within the attorney general's office responsible for leading investigations and presenting cases to judges), judges, prison officials, and treasury and banking officials in charge of tracking the money laundering. They also target those who issue orders and are indirectly responsible for enforcement officers in the field, such as governors, mayors, and agency directors.

Ensuring that public officials responsible for enforcing drug trafficking laws do not comply with those tasks encompasses a wide range of activities. For example, the task of the head of Mexico's Interpol office at the Mexico City airport working for the Sinaloa cartel was to "entertain his people"—the rest of the officials of Interpol—so as to allow certain persons and merchandise to pass through airport security without detection.[17] Other pivotal and more active functions include channeling intelligence information about upcoming government enforcement operations to cartel leaders, offering advanced warning of raids and searches, and providing cover and protection for the movement of cartel leaders and merchandise. The August 2002 arrest of drug trafficker Delia Patricia Buendía Gutiérrez (a.k.a. Ma Baker) revealed that federal police actually picked up cocaine shipments from the planes and delivered them.[18] In this sense, corruption facilitates the everyday operation of the illegal narcotics business. This pattern of corruption also includes the placement of select personnel in key government posts. According to one protected witness, the Sinaloa cartel provided funds to the ex-inspector of the federal police, Edgar Bayardo, to acquire promotions for key allies working within the police agency.[19]

Beyond merely neutralizing law enforcement, corruption is also used by criminal organizations to employ state officials as allies in their fight against the state itself and against rival organizations. By engaging in this type of

> FEDERAL POLICE ACTUALLY PICKED UP COCAINE SHIPMENTS FROM THE PLANES AND DELIVERED THEM.

corruption, state officials move past simple noncompliance into a form of targeted compliance. This is a dramatic shift in the pattern of corruption with public officials proactively abusing state authority in pursuit of the objectives of the criminal organizations. The former police commander in the pay of the Beltrán Leyva cartel noted earlier, for instance, participated in operations against rival groups like the Zetas.[20] In fact, the June 2008 arrest of Colombian trafficker Eder Villafañe was the product of information provided to the government by the Sinaloa cartel.[21] As is discussed later, this has had a tremendous impact on the overall level of violence in Mexico.[22]

A prominent underlying pattern of corruption involves a type of revolving door—somewhat reminiscent of the relationship linking lobbyists to the U.S. Congress, but with far more violent consequences—whereby state security officials leave government service to work for the cartels and cartel members infiltrate and work within the government. Indeed, many cartel leaders and, it seems, most of the *sicarios* (enforcers or hitmen) were once government employees. Mexico's first racketeer, Colonel Esteban Cantú, was a career soldier; one of the first cartel leaders, Miguel Ángel Félix Gallardo, was a former member of the state judicial police; Osiel Cárdenas Guillén of the Gulf cartel was a former federal judicial police officer; Rafael Aguilar Guajardo, who founded the Juárez cartel, was a former commander of the federal police; Amado Carrillo, who made the Juárez cartel famous, was a former police officer; and Arturo Guzmán Decena of the Zetas organization, initially linked to the Gulf cartel, was a former lieutenant in the army's airmobile division of special forces (GAFE).[23] In fact, many of the members of the violent Zetas organization acquired their skills in GAFE and the Mexican military. Lacey estimates that from 2002 to 2009, 100,000 soldiers quit to join

LIKE OTHER CRIMES, CORRUPTION GOES LARGELY UNDETECTED AND UNPUNISHED.

cartels.[24] Bailey and Taylor suggest that as many as one-third of traffickers have served in the military.[25]

While it is difficult to determine corruption's precise role in shaping impunity because Mexico's system of justice suffers from numerous inefficiencies, widespread impunity nonetheless further undermines the efforts of law enforcement. Guillermo Zepeda's extensive study found that only 10 percent of reported crimes end with any formal charges being brought by the public ministry before a judge (and fewer than half of crimes are reported due to lack of trust in the institutions), and even fewer still result in a sentence, resulting in a roughly 97 percent rate of impunity.[26] A more recent report by Human Rights Watch (HRW) shows how the rise in violence has failed to produce a corresponding increase in criminal prosecutions. Of the 35,000 killings the government says were tied to organized crime from December 2007 to January 2011, federal prosecutors opened somewhere between 997 and 1,687 investigations (two different responses were given to HRW by Mexican officials), formally charged 343 suspects, and convicted just 22. HRW noted a similar trend at the state level. From 2009 to 2010 in the state of Chihuahua, there were over 5,000 deaths related to organized crime, but only 212 people were found guilty.[27] Such impunity prompts Bowden to rhetorically ponder: "Imagine living in a place where you can kill anyone you wish and nothing happens except that they fall dead."[28] Like other crimes, corruption goes largely undetected and unpunished. Allegations or even arrests rarely result in prosecution. But even when the enforcement successfully prosecutes traffickers by surmounting the challenges presented by police corruption and impunity, corruption can still provide special privileges and even a means of escape. Corruption in Mexican prisons is widespread. Perhaps the best-known case is the "assisted escape" of the leader of the Sinaloa cartel and one

> BECAUSE OF CORRUPTION, WHEN FIGHTING CRIMINALS, THE STATE MUST ALSO FIGHT PARTS OF ITSELF.

of Forbes's wealthiest individuals, Joaquín "El Chapo" Guzmán, from El Puente Grande maximum-security prison in the state of Jalisco in 2001. The escape revealed an extensive network of payoffs to prison officials that not only allowed for the cartel leader's departure, but for the continued operation of his drug empire from behind bars. This is not the only case of bribery facilitating the release of prisoners, of course. In 2010, over 300 inmates escaped from Mexico's troubled federal prisons, often abetted by officials who allowed prisoners to literally walk out the front door. In one case, prison officials granted inmates an unofficial furlough in order to murder a group of 17 people.[29]

To reiterate, the prevailing patterns of corruption associated with drug trafficking and organized crime not only facilitate the illicit businesses of these organizations, but also effectively handicap official state efforts to control or contain them. Part and parcel of the weaknesses of Mexico's institutions of justice, corruption strips the state of its capacity to enforce the rule of law, gather and effectively use intelligence, carry out investigative and forensic work, make arrests, and prosecute members of criminal organizations or corrupt state officials: in short, to employ the justice system to provide security and accountability. Furthermore, corruption undermines the public's trust in the government and thus prevents the state from receiving the level of cooperation needed from society for effective law enforcement. Thus, because of corruption, when fighting criminals, the state must also fight parts of itself.[30] Understanding the prevailing corrupt bargain is a critical point in understanding both the tools at Calderón's disposal when he launched the 2006 war and the dynamics that war unleashed.

CHANGE VERSUS CONTINUITY

Neither drug trafficking nor corruption in Mexico is new. Both share a long and shadowy history. Yet the violence, brutality, and public insecurity of recent years are qualitatively different. As Howard Campbell points out, "During the PRI's [*Partido Revolucionario Institucional*] 71-year reign, Mexico suffered from endemic corruption and drug trafficking flourished, but at least there was a type of stability, since a small group of powerful traffickers and PRI government officials maintained relatively predictable relationships."[31] Hence the historical paradox: whereas corruption once coexisted and seemingly facilitated the peaceful operation of drug trafficking in Mexico, today it coexists with and arguably facilitates a far more violent species of drug trafficking. This paradox can be explained by three broad changes, which together altered the patterns and impact of corruption as it relates to drug trafficking and organized crime: Mexico's political transformation, changes within the drug trafficking sector itself, and the confrontational policies of President Calderón.

The first monumental change centers on Mexico's political transformation over the course of the past two or three decades—specifically, the dismantling of the PRI-led authoritarian regime. The PRI, as noted, once coordinated a network of informal institutions that essentially governed or managed the relationships linking drug traffickers to the state.[32] As George Grayson points out, "Relying on bribes or *mordidas,* the *desperados* [bandits] pursued their illicit activities with the connivance of authorities [...] Drug dealers behaved discretely, showed deference to public figures, spurned kidnapping, appeared with governors at their children's weddings, and, although often allergic to politics, helped the hegemonic PRI discredit its opponents by linking them to narco-trafficking."[33] Indeed, Kenny and Serrano describe the long disbanded Federal Security Directorate (DFS) as "the country's [first] major criminal mafia."[34] Throughout the 1980s and 1990s, however, opposition parties began to capture control of state and local governments, challenging PRI's hegemony. This undermined the ability of a centralized state to guarantee its side of the corrupt bargain. As local power increasingly fell outside the PRI-controlled networks, federal agents, local police, and corrupt officials all began acting more and more autonomously.[35]

A second area of change occurring during this same period relates to the nature of the Mexican drug business itself. In the 1980s, in response to the U.S. government's efforts to upset the Colombian supply chain through South Florida, the Colombian cartels turned to Mexican suppliers as allies. This sparked a dramatic growth in Mexican operations and profits during a period of peak demand in the United States.[36] Years later, NAFTA further eased the transshipment of drugs into the U.S. market from Mexico, solidly establishing the Mexican cartels as major players.[37] By the turn of the century, over 70 percent of cocaine and a large portion of the marijuana entering the U.S. market were coming through Mexico.[38] Together, these changes channeled vast fortunes to the growing Mexican drug-trafficking organizations, augmenting their autonomy, their numbers, and the level of competition among them.[39] As competition grew, the drug-trafficking organizations began to "vie for influence at both the national and subnational level."[40] Together, the altered political context and the enhanced competition over the lucrative drug market made the organizations more violent.[41] The elimination in 2004 of the ban on assault weapons in the United States, in turn, helped fuel and escalate that violence.

Even prior to the launching of Calderón's war in 2006, these two trends—the erosion of the centralized, authoritarian state and the growing number and power of criminal organizations—had effectively altered the prevailing pattern of drug-related corruption. Rather than the more stabilizing forms of extortion that characterized the PRI period—what Kenny and Serrano refer to as "elite–exploitative" relations in which local political actors essentially held the upper hand—bribery and the colonization of segments of the state by criminal organizations grew to become the dominant pattern.[42] Now, rather than centralized political authorities essentially "managing" the drug businesses and keeping the criminal organizations and the violence within certain bounds, as had occurred under the PRI, the organizations increasingly called the shots, dictating the terms of the relationship and, in turn, increasingly limiting the scope and power of the State. As O'Neil notes, "[Under Fox,] drug-trafficking organizations took advantage of the political opening to gain autonomy, ending their subordination to the government."[43]

Viewed from a slightly different angle, the political fluidity of this period undermined old bargains and the informal rules of operation. This left cartels without the secure state-sponsored protection they had once enjoyed and forced them to acquire their own means of protection and to create their own paramilitary structures.[44] The breakdown of old bargains also prompted the criminal organizations to seek out new allies within the state and to forge new pacts. But while political decentralization broadened the number of potential state allies that could be bought off, it also provided fewer and less reliable returns or guarantees to the drug trafficking organization in exchange for their bribes.[45] This introduced greater uncertainty and risks, feeding the tendency to use violence.

As a result of these underlying changes, the level of violence ratcheted upward during the 1990s and early 2000s. But it was Calderón's militant crackdown—which began on 11 December 2006 when the newly (s)elected president sent 7,000 troops, marines, and federal police to occupy his home state of Michoacán—that would exacerbate these trends. During the ensuing five years as part of his war on drug trafficking organizations, security spending soared, the militarization of law enforcement agencies that had begun under President Zedillo in the late 1990s reached new highs, and the number of arrests, killings, and extraditions of cartel members skyrocketed. The size of the PGR grew from around 21,000 in 2008 to over 26,000 agents by 2010. Between 2001 and 2009, personnel at the public security secretariat more than doubled from 16,810 to 39,840 personnel and grew another 18 percent in 2010. The budget rubric "Order, Security, and Justice" climbed from $3.9 billion in 2003 to $6.8 billion in 2010. The size of the Mexican military also more than doubled from 102,975 members in 1980 to 258,875 in 2010. In Calderón's first budget in 2007, military spending climbed 25 percent and another 13 percent the following year.[46] According to *México Evalúa* (Mexico Evaluation), overall public security spending increased seven times faster under Calderón than it had under the Fox administration.[47] At the same time, the number of extraditions of cartel leaders to the United States climbed from 15 in 2000 to 63 in 2006, 95 in 2008, and 100 by November of 2009.[48]

In addition to strengthening its fight against drug trafficking organizations, in this two-front war, the Calderón government also battled itself. The government initiated a series of reforms designed to enhance the level of cooperation among the over 1,600 law enforcement agencies throughout the country, and to purge and professionalize federal, state, and local police, customs officials, and others. At the same time, it detained and/or replaced numerous officials involved in the war. In 2009, as noted earlier, 357 Mexican law enforcement officers were detained, 90 percent of whom belonged to local police forces.[49] That same year, the customs service replaced all of its 700 inspectors with new agents trained to detect smuggling.[50] In August 2010, the Federal Police dismissed 3,200 agents for failure to conform to internal norms such as passing exams that test honesty and reliability. According to the secretary of public security, by September 2010 a total of 1.2 million police officers from city, state, and federal forces had been removed from their posts during the preceding four years.[51] Within just months after taking office in April 2011, the new attorney general, Marisela Morales, fired 140 federal police officers and investigators and opened more than 280 internal investigations. In August 2011, 21 top federal prosecutors in 21 states and federal districts quit rather than face the internal cleansing.[52] Morales announced in mid-November that 1,500 federal security agents would be dismissed by December. She also claimed that 300 officers had already been released, while 600 were in the process of being removed, and an additional 600 had resigned to avoid processing. The report added that 20,000 employees of the PGR would be vetted through drug tests, lie detectors, and psychological exams.[53]

But despite the increased spending and emboldened enforcement efforts against organized crime and initiatives to fight the debilitating effects of corruption, the level of violence, and arguably corruption, skyrocketed. Amid already intensified competition among criminal organizations, the arrest or killings of cartel leaders by the state merely expanded the power vacuums, unleashing an unprecedented wave of violence among and within the organizations and, to a lesser degree, against state officials.[54] From December 2006 through December 2011, more than 45,000 people have been killed in cartel-related violence.[55] Amid this volatile setting, the nation's criminal organizations unleashed a multi-front war against Calderón's increasingly aggressive and militarized state, on the one hand, and a growing number of splinter and rival organizations (and their armies of state allies) on the other. This multi-front war intensified the need for organized crime to infiltrate the state via corruption to maintain the operation of the primary business (moving drugs into the United States), and for offensive (aggressively expand their territory) and defensive (fending off the government and rivals) purposes. Corrupt allies become even more crucial in providing information about the activities of both a more aggressive state and rival organizations, and as a means to channel information to garner state assistance in fighting their rivals.

Part of this multi-front war involves the state. Though difficult to decipher, violence against the state has come to focus in part on pressuring or intimidating the government in an effort to shift its enforcement attention elsewhere and to target corrupt state officials working for rival organizations. According to Bailey and Taylor, "Mexican gangs' choice of confrontation is aimed primarily at eliminating specific obstacles to their growth or threats to their survival, whether these come from government, rival criminal gangs, or both."[56] Beyond the killing of police and military personnel, violence against the state has come to target mayors, candidates for public office, and others. The year 2010 in particular witnessed the assassination of the gubernatorial candidate in Tamaulipas, Rodolfo Torre Cantú of the PRI, and 15 mayors across the country.[57]

From the perspective of the state, it too faces a multi-front war, both against itself (because of corruption) and against powerful criminal organizations (which are empowered by corruption). Increased enforcement efforts against the cartels not only ignite internal power struggles that create and intensify inter- and intracartel violence, but also strengthen the need for organized crime to corrupt state officials in order to survive. While growing corruption further handicaps the state's enforcement efforts, the growing level of impunity brought about by soaring violence and corruption pushes open the gates ever wider for the pervasive use of violence to settle everyday societal problems. As a result, the state grows increasingly ineffective and unable to fulfill its primary task of providing security, often creating by its actions the exact opposite. At the same time, the state itself becomes a target. As Freeman notes, "anything public servants do that is interpreted as benefiting one group—such as trying to take down its rival—makes them the target of the other."[58] Louise Shelley highlights the inherent paradox here: that combating one or two organizations only strengthens the capacity of their rivals, but launching a simultaneous attack on all is beyond the state's capacity.[59] According to Vanda Falbab-Brown, Mexico, unlike Colombia, is battling six large cartels simultaneously and is unable to destroy any of them because it is spread too thin and because it cannot manage the splinter groups arising from the inter- and intracartel clashes.[60]

In sum, we find that an increased enforcement effort (Calderón's war) undertaken without the appropriate institutional tools to do so has inadvertently increased the overall level of violence and brutality and, arguably, the scope of corruption and degree of impunity in Mexico. But the unintended consequences may extend even further. The current situation has pushed criminal organizations to expand their reach both in terms of their money-making operations and in terms of corruption and violence. Organizations have moved into areas such as kidnapping, human trafficking, the protection/extortion racket (*derecho de piso*), theft and transshipment to the United States of pirated products including stolen petroleum from PEMEX, Mexico's state-owned petroleum company, and, perhaps most problematic, legitimate business efforts.[61] They have expanded operations into Central America and other regions while at the same time reaching further and deeper into Mexican politics. As with most large, well-organized, and well-financed organizations, Mexican-organized criminal groups will continue to seek to assert political and economic influence. They will do so using employment opportunities for Mexico's vast unemployed and underemployed population, campaign contributions to candidates, and corrupt payoffs to state officials if possible, and—as shown by the killings of local and state candidates, and perhaps even key officials in the Calderón government—violence and intimidation if necessary.[62]

CONCLUSION

Mexico suffers a glaring "rule of law deficit." State institutions lack the capacity to enforce the law vis-à-vis society and vis-à-vis themselves. In the past, seemingly strong informal institutions either hid these shortcomings or minimized their effects. But recent experience shows that launching a war against powerful drug traffickers and criminal organizations without the capacity to adequately do so leaves the state with few tools but force itself, resulting in a spiral of violence and an unprecedented level of insecurity. Such a setting makes for a less than propitious moment to try to address deep-seated corruption or professionalize faulty institutions. The lack of respect for the government and the law, in turn, leaves the government largely isolated and lacking the degree of cooperation from society needed to execute the war and enforce the rule of law. Poverty and inequality complicate these tasks even more by providing criminal organizations with a ready and willing army of labor and victims and by further isolating the government. Meanwhile, the United States' huge supply of arms and demand for drugs seem to pull the country excruciatingly in opposing directions. Ultimately, it is not entirely clear how far—or high—the drug-trafficking-related corruption reaches, how to escape this quagmire, or how a change in presidential administrations in December 2012 might have an impact.[63] It seems certain given the results of the Calderón war that the country will most likely seek a strategy that focuses more on reducing the level of violence rather than on crippling drug trafficking, addresses the underlying social and economic causes, and relies less on violent confrontation.

NOTES

1. "Murder of Mexican Activist Sparks Corruption Claims," *New Zealand Herald,* December 1, 2011, http://www.nzherald.co.nz/murder20of20mexican20activ-ist/search/results.cfm?kw1=Murder%20of%20Mexican%20Activist&kw2 =&st=gsa.

2. Peter Andreas, "The Political Economy of Narco-Corruption in Mexico," *Current History* (April, 1998): 160–65; June S. Beittel, *Mexico's Drug Trafficking Organizations: Source and Scope of the Rising Violence,* Congressional Research Service (CRS) Report for Congress, 7–7500 (June 7, 2011); Stephanie Hanson, "Mexico's Drug War," Council on Foreign Relations (November 20, 2008); Thomas R. Naylor, "Predators, Parasites, of Free-Market Pioneers: Reflections on the Nature and Analysis of Profit-Driven Crime," in *Critical Reflections on Transnational Organized Crime, Money Laundering, and Corruption,* ed. Margaret E. Beare (Toronto: University of Toronto Press, 2003), 35–54; Thomas R. Naylor, "Violence and Illegal Economic Activity: A Deconstruction," *Crime, Law and Social Change* 52 (2009): 231–42; Patrick O'Day and Angelina López, "Organizing the Underground NAFTA," *Journal of Contemporary Criminal Justice* 17, no. 3 (2001): 232–42; Stanley A. Pimental, "Mexico's Legacy of Corruption," in *Menace to Society: Political Criminal Collaboration around the World,* ed. Roy Godson (Piscataway, NJ: Transaction, 2003), 175–98; Louise Shelley, "The Unholy Trinity: Transnational Crime, Corruption, and Terrorism," *Brown Journal of World Affairs* 11, no. 2 (2005): 101–11.

3. Naylor, "Predators, Parasites, of Free-Market Pioneers," 35–54.

4. Laurie Freeman, "State of Siege: Drug-Related Violence and Corruption in Mexico," WOLA Special Report (June 2006), 12. Despite the almost axiomatic connection tying drug-trafficking and corruption, the direction of causality is not entirely clear. It may, of course, move in both directions. One prominent view suggests that organized crime corrupts state officials through the seductive power of bribes (that organized crime à corruption). But, as Peter Andreas ("The Political Economy of Narco-Corruption," 161) points

out, corruption is a two-way street and "involves not only the penetration of the state, but also penetration by the state." A second view thus reverses the direction of causality and depicts corruption as the independent variable that produces and hence promotes drug trafficking operations (corruption à organized crime).

5. Sergio Javier Jiménez and Silvia Otero, "Todos somos responsables de la inseguridad: Calderón," *El Univeral*, August 21, 2008, www.eluniversal.com.mx/notas/531961.html.

6. *Justice in Mexico*, Monthly News Report, November 2009, 8–9.

7. Gustavo Castillo García, "Noé Ramírez recibía del *cártel* de Sinaloa 450 mil dólares al mes, reveló Medina Mora," *La Jornada*, December 22, 2008, www.jornada.unam.mx/2008/11/22/index.php?section=politica&article=011n1pol. See also: David Aponte, *Los Infiltrados: El narco dentro de los gobiernos* (Mexico City, DF: Grijalbo, 2011).

8. University of San Diego: Trans-Border Institute, "Justice in Mexico: October 2010 Monthly News Report," http://justiceinmexico.files.wordpress.com/2010/11/2010-10-october_news_report.pdf, 16.

9. University of San Diego: Trans-Border Institute, "Justice in Mexico: June 2010 Monthly News Report," http://catcher.sandiego.edu/items/peacestudies/June2010.pdf, 10–1.

10. Paul Kenny and Monica Serrano, ed., *Mexico's Security Failure: Collapse into Criminal Violence* (New York: Routledge, 2011), 33.

11. Antonio Baranda and Rolando Herrera, "Halla narco socio dentro de Policía," *Reforma*, September 25, 2009.

12. *Justice in Mexico*, Monthly News Report, November 2009, 10.

13. Daniel A. Sabet, "Confrontation, Collusion, and Tolerance: The Relationship between Law Enforcement and Organized Crime in Tijuana," *Mexican Law Review* 2, no. 2 (2010): 3–29.

14. Charles Bowden, *Murder City: Ciudad Juárez and the Global Economy's New Killing Fields* (New York: Nation Books, 2010), 109.

15. Paul Kenny and Monica Serrano, ed. *Mexico's Security Failure: Collapse into Criminal Violence* (New York: Routledge, 2011), 41.

16. Alma Guillermoprieto, "The Murderers of Mexico," *New York Review of Books*, October 28, 2010.

17. Aponte, *Los Infiltrados*, 20.

18. Raúl Monge, "La estructura policiaca al servicio de 'ma baker'," *Proceso* 1348 (September 1, 2002).

19. Aponte, *Los Infiltrados*, 141.

20. Ibid.

21. Ibid., 144.

22. J. Jesús Esquivel, "'El Vicentillo', asunto de seguridad nacional en Estados Unidos," *Proceso* 1830 (December 14, 2011), 14–15; Alberto M. Osorio and Felipe Cobian R., "Y el paraíso tapatío se derrumbó," *Proceso* 1820 (September 18, 2011); Andrew Kennis and Jason McGahan, "Rapido y furiosos: Armas para 'El Chapo,'" *Proceso* 1820 (September 18, 2011). A frequently voiced hypothesis in Mexico suggests that just like other corrupt officials, President Calderón is siding with a particular organization (the Sinaloa cartel) and targeting enforcement measures accordingly. Recent reports point to the possibility that the United States has also been helping the Sinaloan cartel through its Fast and Furious program and money laundering schemes.

23. Kenny and Serrano, *Security Failure*, 29.

24. Marc Lacey, "In an Escalating War, Mexico Fights the Cartels, and Itself," *New York Times*, March 30, 2011.

25. John Bailey and Matthew M. Taylor, "Evade, Corrupt, or Confront? Organized Crime and the State in Brazil and Mexico," *Journal of Politics in Latin America* (2009): 19; Aponte, *Los Infiltrados*. It should be pointed out that corruption moves in a variety of directions. Just as drug traffickers pay off police, one of the state's major investigative tools—and the source of much inside information on corruption—involves police payoffs (sometimes in the form of immunity and new identities) to members of drug trafficking organizations in exchange for information, particularly following their arrest. The testimony of "Felipe" for example, a former official who had infiltrated the U.S. embassy in Mexico, was key to the arrests of key SIEDO officials in *Operación Limpieza* (see: Aponte, *Los Infiltrados*).

26. Guillermo Zepeda Lecuona, *Crimen sin castigo: Procuración de justicia penal y Ministerio Público en México* (Mexico City, D.F.: Centro de Investigación para el Desarrollo and Fondo de Cultura Económica).

27. Human Rights Watch, *Mexico: Neither Rights Nor Security: Killings, Torture, and Disappearances in Mexico's 'War on Drugs,'* www.hrw.org/reports/2011/11/09/neither-rights-nor-security-0, 171.

28. Bowden, *Murder City*, 13.

29. Vidriana Rios and David A. Shirk, *Drug Violence in Mexico: Data and Analysis through 2010*, (San Diego: University of San Diego, 2010), 16–17.

30. Kenny and Serrano, *Security Failure*, 29.

31. Howard Campbell, *Drug War Zone: Frontline Dispatches from the Streets of El Paso and Juárez* (Austin: University of Texas Press, 2009), 271.

32. Louise Shelley, "Confrontation, Collusion, and Tolerance: The Relationship between Law Enforcement and Organized Crime in Tijuana," *Brown Journal of World Affairs* 11, no. 2 (2005): 215.

33. George Grayson, *Mexico: Narco-Violence and a Failed State?* (New Brunswick: Transaction, 2010), 29.

34. Kenny and Serrano, *Security Failure*, 33.

35. Grayson, *Mexico*, 31.

36. Carpenter, *Foreign Policy Briefing*, 87.

37. Grayson, *Mexico*, 56.

38. Intelligence Center, *National Drug Threat Assessment 2005*, February 2005.

39. Grayson, *Mexico*, 31.

40. Rios and Shirk, *Drug Violence*, 11.

41. Grayson, *Mexico*, 31.

42. Kenny and Serrano, *Mexico's Security Failure*, 33.

43. Shannon O'Neil, "The Real War in Mexico," *Foreign Affairs* 88, no. 4 (2009): 63–77.

44. Richard Snyder and Angelica Duran-Martínez, "Does Illegality Breed Violence? Drug Trafficking and State-Sponsored Protection Rackets," *Crime, Law, and Social Change* 52 (2009): 264.

45. Ibid.

46. Juan Lindau, "The Drug War's Impact on Executive Power, Judicial Reform, and Federalism in Mexico," *Political Science Quarterly* 126 (2011): 177–200.

47. University of San Diego: Trans-Border Institute, "Justice in Mexico: August 2011 Monthly News Report," http://justiceinmexico.files.wordpress.com/2011/02/2011-08-august-news-report.pdf, 7–8.

48. University of San Diego: Trans-Border Institute, "Justice in Mexico: November 2009 Monthly News Report," http://catcher.sandiego.edu/items/peacestudies/JMPnovember2009.pdf, 4–5.

49. Baranda and Herrera,"Halla narco socio dentro de Policía," *Reforma*, September 25, 2009.

50. University of San Diego: Trans-Border Institute, "Justice in Mexico: August 2009 Monthly News Report," http://catcher.sandiego.edu/items/peacestudies/JMPaugust2009.pdf, 2.

51. University of San Diego: Trans-Border Institute, "Justice in Mexico: September 2010 Monthly News Report," http://justiceinmexico.files.wordpress.com/2010/10/2010-09-september_news_report1.pdf, 10.

52. Chuck Neubauer, "Mexican prosecutors step down amid purge," *Washington Times*, August 2, 2011.

53. University of San Diego: Trans-Border Institute, "Justice in Mexico: August 2011 Monthly News Report," 4–15.

54. Eduardo Guerreo Gutierrez, "Como reducer la violencia," *Nexos en línea*, November 3, 2010. The most dramatic spike in violence took place between 2008 and 2010. Drug-related executions climbed from 2,500 in 2007 to 5,207 in 2008, to 6,587 in 2009, and to more than 11,800 in 2010. Two waves of violence marked the period. The first took place between May and November in 2008 following the detention of Alfredo Beltrán Leyva (El Mochomo) and the breaking off of relations between the Beltrán Leyva brothers and the Sinaloa cartel. The second wave took place between December 2009 and May 2010 following the death of Arturo Beltrán Leyva (El Barbas) during a military operation.

55. University of San Diego: Trans-Border Institute, "Justice in Mexico: February 2012 Monthly News Report," http://justiceinmexico.files.wordpress.com/2011/02/2012-02-february-news-report.pdf, 7.

56. John Bailey and Matthew M. Taylor, "Evade, Corrupt, or Confront? Organized Crime and the State in Brazil and Mexico," *Journal of Politics in Latin America* 1, no. 2 (2009): 22.

57. Vidriana Rios, "Why are Mexican Mayors Getting Killed by Traffickers? A Model of Competitive Corruption" (Unpublished, 2011).

58. Freeman, "State of Siege," 6.

59. Shelley, "Corruption and Organized Crime in Mexico in the Post-PRI Transition," 214. The government claims that most of the killings (roughly 90 percent) are by drug-traffickers, and that only seven percent are by Mexican security forces. See: June S. Beittel, *Mexico's Drug Trafficking Organizations: Source and Scope of the Rising Violence*, Congressional Research Service Report for Congress, 7–7500 (June 7, 2011), 20. Yet given the lack of investigative prowess on the part of the government, it is unclear exactly how they arrive at this figure. As noted, exceedingly few of these killings have made it through the judicial system. Rúben Aguilar and Jorge G. Castañeda *El Narco: La Guerra Fallida. Mexico: Punto de Lectura*, (Mexico City, D.F.: Santillana Ediciones Generales, 2009) contend that perhaps what the government portrays as violence among drug traffickers may really be the work of state officials. The growing concern, however, is that state violence is being targeted at innocent journalists, human rights activists, students, and other members of society. See: John M. Ackerman, "How Mexico Gets it Wrong," *Los Angeles Times*, March 16, 2010.

60. Vanda Felbab-Brown, "Lessons from Colombia for Mexico? Caveat Emptor," Brookings Institution, in University of San Diego: Trans-Border Institute, "Justice in Mexico: February 2012 Monthly News Report," 4.

61. In October 2011, 121 INM agents were fired for alleged complicity in abduction of Central American migrants. Such abductions, including the mass execution of migrants in the state Tamaulipas, were attributed to the Zeta organization (*Justice in Mexico,* Monthly News Report, October 2011). For information on stolen Petroleum from PEMEX, see: Ana Lilia Pérez, "Los careless, infiltrados en PEMEX," *Proceso* 1832 (December 11, 2011).

62. Speculation persists that the plane crash that took the life of the Interior Secretary and Calderón's most trusted advisor, Juan Camilo Mouriño, along with a top official within the ministry of public security, José Luis Santiago Vasconcelos, in 2008, and the helicopter crash that killed the Interior Secretary José Francisco Blake Mora in November 2011 were not accidents.

63. For one approach to solving the quagmire, see: Universidad Nacional Autónoma de México and Instituto Iberoamericano de Derecho Constitucional, *Elementos para la Construcción de una Política de Estado para la Seguridad y Justicia en Democracia* (August 2011), www.ddu.unam.mx/imgs/Inicio/SeguridadYJusticia/propuesta_s_AGO11.pdf.

three

M exico has suffered staggering levels of violence and crime during the country's seven-year war against the cartels. The fighting has killed 90,000 people so far, a death toll larger than that of the civil war in Syria. Homicide rates have tripled since 2007. In an effort to stem the carnage, Mexican President Enrique Peña Nieto announced last December that the federal government, having struggled to defeat the cartels using corrupt local police and an inadequate military, would create an elite national police force of 10,000 officers by the end of this year. The lawlessness spawned by Mexico's drug wars has contributed to the spread of self-defense groups, and the groups regularly blame the cartels and the government's war on drugs for the lack of security. But they are not concerned mainly with stopping the drug trade. Around the world, community-based crime-fighting groups have sprung up in places where formal security forces are absent or inadequate, often with the approval and support of governments. In this compact essay, two specialists from the Center for Naval Analyses lay out this phenomenon as it applies to Mexico.

THE RISE OF MEXICO'S SELF-DEFENSE FORCES

VIGILANTE JUSTICE SOUTH OF THE BORDER

By Patricio Asfura-Heim and Ralph Espach

O n a Tuesday morning in March, with rifles slung over their shoulders, some 1,500 men filed into the Mexican town of Tierra Colorada, which sits on the highway from Mexico City down to the Pacific coast. They seized at gunpoint 12 police officers and a local security official, whom they believed responsible for the murder of their commander. They set up roadblocks, and when a car of Acapulco-bound beachgoers refused to stop, they opened fire and injured a passenger.

This was not the work of a drug cartel. The men were members of a self-defense group, one of a growing number of vigilante organizations aiming to restore order to Mexican communities. "We have besieged the municipality," said a spokesperson for the group, "because here criminals operate with impunity in broad daylight."

Mexico has suffered staggering levels of violence and crime during the country's seven-year-long war against the cartels. The fighting has killed 90,000 people so far, a death toll larger than that

Patricio Asfura-Heim and Ralph Espach, "The Rise of Mexico's Self-Defense Forces: Vigilante Justice South of the Border," Foreign Affairs, vol. 92, no. 4, pp. 143-150. Copyright © 2013 by Council on Foreign Relations, Inc. Reprinted with permission.

of the civil war in Syria. Homicide rates have tripled since 2007. In an effort to stem the carnage, Mexican President Enrique Peña Nieto announced last December that the federal government, having struggled to defeat the cartels using corrupt local police and an inadequate military, would create an elite national police force of 10,000 officers by the end of this year.

Many Mexicans are unwilling to wait. In communities across the country, groups of men have donned masks, picked up rifles and machetes, and begun patrolling their neighborhoods and farmland. As in the Tierra Colorada incident, their behavior is not always pretty. Several months ago, another such group in the state of Guerrero detained 54 people for over six weeks, accusing them of crimes ranging from stealing cattle to murder. After a series of unofficial trials, they handed 20 of them over to local prosecutors and let the rest go free.

In other communities, detainees have been beaten, forced into labor, or even lynched. Members of these *fuerzas autodefensas* (self-defense forces) say that they have no choice but to take matters into their own hands: criminals and gangs have become more brazen and violent than ever, and the police and the government are either absent, corrupt, or themselves working with the criminals.

Extralegal local self-defense groups have long been common in rural Mexico, particularly in indigenous communities in the south. In recent months, however, such groups have emerged with alarming frequency across the country, suggesting that many Mexicans have lost faith in the government's willingness or ability to protect them. They have formed in the Pacific states of Michoacán and Jalisco, in the northern border state of Chihuahua, in the eastern states of Veracruz and Tabasco, and on the outskirts of Mexico City. They now operate openly in 13 different states and at least 68 municipalities. According to the government, 14 new groups have formed since January; Mexican security analysts say the real number is likely much higher.

The motives of these self-defense groups vary from town to town, as do their relationships with local governments and the police. The majority of them seem to draw on local outrage against the rising crime and violence in their communities. For others, the impetus is less clear. Some may represent instances of political opportunism. One local self-defense force in a small town in Oaxaca dissolved after 48 hours once the state government agreed to improve public services and oversight of the police. In other cases, the groups have taken advantage of political vacuums to advance illicit interests, even working as fronts for local gangs or trafficking networks. La Familia Michoacana, for example, originally claimed that its mission was to fight the Zetas and other drug cartels—and then became a drug cartel itself. These groups often consist of well-intentioned citizens, unknowing pawns in a criminal network's scheme to hobble a rival.

The lawlessness spawned by Mexico's drug wars has contributed to the spread of self-defense groups, and the groups regularly blame the cartels and the government's war on drugs for the lack of security. But they are not mainly concerned with stopping the drug trade. With a few exceptions, such as the Mata Zetas (Zeta Killers) in Monterrey, their focus tends to be on local crimes, particularly robberies, rapes, and other violent attacks. Their actions have until now been limited to seizing alleged delinquents and criminals and either punishing them publicly or handing them over to the police. As one group leader in Tierra Colorada explained, "Narcotraffickers as a rule usually keep things under control in their territories, but lately they've been getting involved in extortion and murders, and that's not right. The drug problem is for the state to resolve, but kidnapping and robbery touches us."

The rapid proliferation of these groups poses a challenge to the Peña Nieto government just as it is trying to reform Mexico's security policies. In a basic way, armed extralegal groups undermine the formal rule of law, and left unchecked, they could morph into criminal organizations themselves. But they have long played a role Mexico and in many regions enjoy a degree of public legitimacy that the police lack. Rather than try to dissolve these forces, Mexican officials must discern between those acting legitimately with local public support and those with ulterior motives and seek ways in which the former can contribute to public security—at least until the government gets its act together.

GRASS-ROOTS SECURITY

Around the world, community-based crime-fighting groups have sprung up in places where formal security forces are absent or inadequate, often with the approval and support of governments. Despite their sometimes noble intentions, these organizations can pose a challenge to the authority and legitimacy of the state. In some cases when they have operated without oversight, they have killed wantonly, displaced thousands from their lands, or themselves taken up crime. The United Self-Defense Forces of Colombia, for example, came into existence purportedly to protect rural communities from the Revolutionary Armed Forces of Colombia, or FARC, but transformed over time into a paramilitary network that committed massacres, trafficked drugs, and engaged in corruption at the highest levels. Self-defense groups have often proved vulnerable to co-optation by criminal and insurgent groups.

Policymakers and academics alike tend to disdain less-than-official security arrangements, associating them with lawlessness and the decay of a state's monopoly on coercive power. They often conflate grass-roots policing with rogue, power-hungry militias or paramilitary forces. Indeed, the line between the two can often be a fine one. Groups that set out to protect their communities may simultaneously infringe on the well-being of neighboring populations.

Yet it would be wrong to dismiss the utility of these types of groups altogether, particularly in an age rife with civil conflict. A growing body of research suggests that when states are unable or unwilling to provide security, local self-defense groups may be an imperfect but effective alternative. These forces are much cheaper and faster to assemble than formal police and army units, and they can quickly muster large numbers of men to secure isolated communities. Whereas outside forces need years to get to know the geography and residents of an area, local self-defense groups start with a leg up. Moreover, since these groups are motivated to protect their families and communities, they tend to be less predatory and to have higher morale than state security forces. In places as diverse as Afghanistan and Sierra Leone, such groups are often held in check by community leaders and remain in large part dependent on their neighbors for information and material support. Finally, when the state cooperates with self-defense groups, it can use those ties to reach out to isolated communities and provide them with public services.

As cases from around the world show, these groups can be useful especially when governments incorporate them into a broader and well-formulated security strategy. In the 1980s and 1990s, when the Indian state of Punjab was rocked by a Sikh insurgency, the police were able to quell the unrest by coordinating with a large, well-organized, and well-supported volunteer force. At its peak, the Village Defense Scheme included nearly 1,100 village committees and 40,000 men. This force was completely integrated into the Punjab police's overall counterinsurgency strategy. The police trained the volunteer units, assigned small detachments to support them, and worked with them to draw up village defense plans. Unlike those in Mexico, this self-defense force was organized by the government, but its success nonetheless demonstrates that states can make good use of informal security organizations.

Around the same time, when Peru faced a brutal Maoist guerilla movement known as the Shining Path, the country's local self-defense and development committees played a major role in protecting the population in the rural highlands and enabling aid to flow there. Once they had served their purpose, the groups were able to integrate into Peruvian society. Several peasant commanders demobilized and transformed their units into political organizations that continue to work on behalf of the indigenous population. Other groups remain active and still useful: the current government in Lima has recently pledged to work with them on stopping drug trafficking and crime.

SAFETY FIRST

The rise of self-defense groups has provoked a fierce debate in Mexico. Many Mexicans fear that if the groups are allowed to operate, they could exacerbate the violence, undermine the rule of law, violate citizens' rights, and spread crime. In February, the governor of the state of Sinaloa said that the legalization of these groups would amount to an admission of state failure. That same month, Manuel Mondragón y Kalb, the director of the National Security Commission, echoed these concerns, arguing that organized crime and the drug cartels appear to be "the hand that rocks the cradle" of the self-defense forces. Others accept that they are necessary so long as Mexican communities remain unsafe. The governor of Michoacán, for example, has pledged to support self-defense groups in his state with formal police training and equipment.

The critics are right that the ultimate solution to Mexico's struggle against organized crime lies in the modernization of its security sector. But in the near term, the Mexican government may not have the ability or the will to effect dramatic institutional changes, such as creating more effective police forces. Until it does, policymakers cannot overlook the immediate need to keep the country's communities safe. When the time comes, demobilizing the community groups will prove tricky and time consuming. But it can be achieved through a variety of inducements, including paying the vigilantes, finding them jobs, and integrating the groups into regular security forces.

> IT WOULD BE WRONG TO DISMISS THE UTILITY OF SELF-DEFENSE GROUPS ALTOGETHER, PARTICULARLY IN AN AGE RIFE WITH CIVIL CONFLICT.

Meanwhile, the spread of these groups indicates that the idea of community defense may be gaining in popularity. Although the federal government officially refuses to recognize the groups, several state and local governments have. Some have negotiated agreements with the community forces, some have provided them with training and basic equipment, and others simply permit them to exist and operate, hoping undue trouble does not arise.

The Peña Nieto administration is rightly focused on creating a new national police force, professionalizing Mexico's local police, and improving its judicial and penal systems. But these reforms will take years, if not decades. And for the moment, the government has few good options for stemming the proliferation of community self-defense groups. Mexico could dispatch its police and armed forces to break up the groups, but doing so would divert precious resources away from the fight against cartels and criminals. Such an approach could also stoke even more local outrage against the government and either radicalize these community groups or encourage them to seek accommodation with other shadowy organizations that promise to provide security.

A better approach would be to reach out to the community self-defense forces and create positive relationships between them and the local or federal police. In fact, these kinds of arrangements are not uncommon. Since 1995, more than 80 villages in Guerrero have administered their own police and justice systems, following traditional indigenous practices, within the state-sponsored Regional Coordinator of Community Authorities program. This program has created units that are composed of armed villagers who perform routine patrols and turn suspects over to town assemblies. The state government gives them a small amount of training, simple T-shirt uniforms, and the authority to solve certain types of disputes.

Mexico must study the successful models from around the world to understand how coordination between formal and informal security forces can keep communities safe while still allowing for justice, accountability, and the rule of law. In the best cases, such cooperation has involved direct oversight of self-defense forces by a competent formal security force, a simultaneous focus on local economic development so that community defense does not evolve into mercenary activity, and efforts to restrict the armaments and geographic range of the voluntary forces to ensure that they operate only in a defensive capacity. As Mexico continues to reform and professionalize its law enforcement institutions—a project that is still years from bearing fruit—a flexible and pragmatic approach to self-defense groups will best serve the country.

four

This reading examines the changing roles of Central American gangs within the drug trafficking structures, particularly the Mexican drug trafficking organizations (DTOs) operating in the region. This will include the emerging political role of the gangs (Mara Salvatrucha, or MS-13, as well as Barrio 18), the negotiations between the gangs and Mexican DTOs for joint operational capacity, the interactions between the two sides, and the significant repercussions all these will likely have across the region as the gangs become both better financed and more politically aware and active. This article is based on field research in San Salvador, where Douglas Farah was able to spend time with some members of MS-13. It is also informed by his examination of the truce between the gangs and the Salvadoran government as well as the talks between the gangs and the Sinaloa Cartel.[1] *In the second article*, Duncan Breda and I examine the current gang situation in El Salvador, Honduras, and Guatemala and in particular the reform efforts undertaken by each of the governments over the past couple of years.

CENTRAL AMERICAN GANGS

CHANGING NATURE AND NEW PARTNERS

By Douglas Farah

C entral America's geographic location—between the world's
largest cocaine producers in Colombia, Bolivia, and Peru
and the world's largest market in the United States—has made it a
strategic transit route for illicit drugs for more than three decades.
While the region has been of constant interest to transnational
criminal organizations (TCOs), in recent years, its importance as
a transshipment route has grown dramatically. During the 1990s,
only about 30 percent of the cocaine from South America for the
U.S. market transited through Central America; current estimates
indicate that up to 90 percent now moves through the region.[2]

This shift in drug routes, brought on in part by successful U.S.
and Caribbean efforts to crimp the sea traffic that funneled illicit
drugs into Miami, has coincided with a significant rise in violence
in Central America's Northern Triangle: Honduras, El Salvador,
and Guatemala. Most of the violence is attributed to powerful
gangs, known as *maras* or *pandillas*, which have taken over territory

Douglas Farah, "Central American Gangs: Changing Nature and New Partners,"
Journal of International Affairs, vol. 66, no. 1, pp. 53-67. Copyright © 2012 by The
Journal of International Affairs. Reprinted with permission. Provided by ProQuest LLC.

> GLOBAL ILLICIT TRADE IS
> SINKING ENTIRE INDUSTRIES
> WHILE BOOSTING OTHERS,
> RAVAGING COUNTRIES AND
> SPARKING BOOMS, MAKING
> AND BREAKING POLITICAL
> CAREERS, DESTABILIZING
> SOME GOVERNMENTS AND
> PROPPING UP OTHERS.

and petty crime activity throughout the region.

There is significant debate within the law enforcement, intelligence, and development communities over the true nature of the ties between local gangs and larger TCOs. The recent truce between El Salvador's two main gangs, Mara Salvatrucha (MS-13) and Calle 18, brokered by government-sanctioned intermediaries, has brought heightened attention to the phenomenon of Central American gangs, their relationship with TCOs, and the role they are beginning to play in national and local politics.[3]

This paper examines the changing nature of the gangs, particularly in El Salvador, their strengthening ties to TCOs, especially the Mexican Sinaloa and Los Zetas drug cartels, their independent human trafficking structures, and finally, the implications these developments have for the arc of transnational criminal activity across Central America, Mexico, and the United States.

This paper will also examine the new inroads that gangs have made in becoming recognized political forces through their control of extensive territory in the countries where they operate and their ability to negotiate with the government for concessions and benefits. It is part of a broader trend aptly described by Moisés Naím in his seminal book, *Illicit*, about the unintended consequences of globalization and the growth of transnational organized crime:

> Ultimately it is the fabric of society that is at stake. Global illicit trade is sinking entire industries while boosting others, ravaging countries and sparking booms, making and breaking political careers, destabilizing some governments and propping up others. At one extreme are countries where the smuggling routes, the

hidden factories, the pilfered natural resources, the dirty-money transactions can no longer be distinguished from the official economy and government. But comfortable middle-class lives in wealthy countries are far more connected to trafficking—and to its global effects—than most of us care to imagine.[4]

Much of the research for this paper was conducted through interviews with members of MS-13 during seven trips to El Salvador over the past two years. Through trusted intermediaries, whose friendships I have developed during my twenty-seven years of working in the region, I was able to meet with gang members ranging from foot soldiers to the upper level leadership. I visited their neighborhoods, met their families, and established a dialogue with them. I also spent many hours discussing the gang phenomenon with investigators who have been working with the gangs and studying their behavior for years; I am deeply in their debt for the knowledge and insights they have provided. Much of the information here is based on my field work and not on previously published studies. Due to the risk posed to the lives of those who have become my guides in the gang world, my sources are not identified by name.

The gangs, long part of an extremely violent local subculture that operates in the neighborhoods they control and constantly at war with rival gangs, are in a historic process of change. Some investigators such as John Sullivan have already characterized the MS-13 and similar groups as "third-generation gangs" at the forefront of "ushering in an era of asymmetric threats, where nonstate actors can extend their influence and challenge states and their institutions to gain social, political, or economic influence."[5] Other scholars such as Max Manwaring have described gangs as a "new urban insurgency" arguing:

The common denominator that can link gangs to insurgency is that some gangs' and insurgents' ultimate objective is to depose or control the governments of targeted countries. As a consequence, the "Duck Analogy" applies. That is, third generation gangs look like ducks, walk like ducks, and act like ducks—a peculiar breed, but ducks nevertheless![6]

What these prescient analysts did not include was the opportunity for these groups to link their structures to the superstructures of TCOs, a linkage neither smooth nor uniform, but one that is growing in multiple aspects. This change has significant implications, not only within the specific countries where the gangs have their bases of operation, but also for the Central American region and the United States. Ultimately, these changes will impact the future contours of transnational organized crime across the Western Hemisphere.

THE DEVELOPMENT OF THE GANGS

The history of the emergence of violent youth gangs in the northern triangle of Central America during the mid-1990s has been well documented. However, it is worth reviewing briefly, because, without an understanding of how the gangs emerged, it is difficult to understand what the gangs have become, the relationships they have developed, and the current transformation process.

Following the 1992 riots in Los Angeles, prosecutors began to charge young Latino gang members as adults instead of minors, sending hundreds to prison on felony charges. This was followed in 1996 by a national immigration law legislating that noncitizens sentenced to more than a year in

> AS SELF-FINANCING ENTITIES, THE CRIMINAL ENTITIES WERE IDENTIFIED AS HAVING A STRONG ECONOMIC COMPONENT ... RATHER THAN BEING PRIMARILY POLITICAL IN NATURE.

prison would be repatriated to their countries of origin after serving their sentences.[7]

This policy led to the repatriation of tens of thousands of young Central Americans to countries they were unfamiliar with, where many did not even speak the language. In an effort to survive, the deportees, mostly young men, sought social acceptance and safety by banding together and replicating the gang structures they had come out of in the Los Angeles area. From 2000 to 2004, some 20,000 young Central American criminals were deported.[8] The trend accelerated from the early years, and from 2008 to 2010, another 63,000 criminals were deported to El Salvador.[9]

From a Congressional Research Service report, it is reasonable to extrapolate that over the past fifteen years, more than 300,000 criminals, mostly gang members, have been deported to El Salvador, Honduras, Nicaragua, and Guatemala—all countries that were in the process of re-covering from a decade of civil war.[10] Within these countries, police forces were new and untrained, the judicial systems were fragile and often not fully functional, and there was virtually no social safety net in place to deal with the onslaught.

As investigative journalist Ana Arana notes, the consequences have been severe:

Fed by an explosive growth in the area's youth population and by a host of social problems such as poverty and unemployment, the gangs are spreading, spilling into Mexico and beyond—even back into the United States itself. With them, the maras are bringing rampant crime, committing thousands of murders, and contribut-ing to a flourishing drug trade. Central America's governments, meanwhile, seem utterly unable to meet the challenge, lacking the skills, know-how and money necessary to fight these supergangs.[11]

For instance, in El Salvador, the early gang deportees lost little time in making alliances, often for survival, with the enormous pool of demobilized combatants from both sides of the country's civil war. Rather than completely demobilizing, as called for by the peace agreement ending the war, small cadres of these combatants had kept some weaponry, and many were from highly trained special forces units. This allowed these newly formed alliances, almost from their inception, to take control of large swaths of territory.[12]

After the war, the security situation in El Salvador deteriorated so quickly that two years after peace agreements were signed, the United Nations funded a special commission to identify the reasons why "illegal armed groups" operating after the war had "morphed" into more sophisticated, complex organizations than those that had existed during the war. As self-financing entities, the criminal entities were identified as having a strong economic component to their organization and operations, rather than being primarily political in nature.[13]

THE EXPECTATION HELD BY THE GREAT MAJORITY OF THE GANG MEMBERS WAS THAT THEY WOULD BE DEAD OR IN PRISON WITHIN A FEW YEARS.

As the gangs and their intergang battles grew, so did the levels of violence in the countries where they operated. In the absence of strong state institutions, and weariness after the civil wars, these groups were still in the process of finding their footing. These early criminal enterprises operated regionally and were often made up of former combatants who knew and trusted each other from the conflicts. They initially focused on kidnappings and extortion for their income. By the end of the 1990s, however, they were moving into cocaine trafficking as escorts and enforcers for pre-existing Colombian and Mexican TCOs that were primarily involved in drug trafficking.

In addition to their roles as foot soldiers for TCOs, the gangs were also involved in petty crime, such as purse snatching, robbery, taxing bus drivers and small stores in their neighborhoods, as well as small-scale drug distribution in certain parts of the cities in order to keep themselves economically afloat. This quickly led to an escalation in homicide rates, as gang members fought each other over the most economically advantageous territory and sought to expand their geographic influence. The expectation held by the great majority of the gang members was that they would be dead or in prison within a few years; the future held very little hope of survival and almost no hope of ever leaving the gang life alive.[14]

Because of the common origin of many of the gang members and the boom in computer and cell phone technology, gang members could easily stay in touch with each other, whether they were based in El Salvador, Honduras, Guatemala, or the United States. Due to the historically large number of people seeking to leave the region and entering the United States illegally, the MS-13 quickly moved into the human smuggling business for two complementary reasons: to generate funding and to establish lines of movement for themselves across borders with impunity, thus allowing the leadership to remain mobile and hard to arrest. If a hit were to be carried out in El Salvador, often a gang member from Honduras or Guatemala would be brought in to carry out the execution, and then slipped back across the border.[15] As one early study on transnational gangs noted:

> The capacity to cross national borders creates several advantages for criminal networks. It enables them to supply markets where the profit margins are largest, operate from and in countries where risks are the least, complicate the tasks of law enforcement agencies that are trying to combat them, commit crimes that cross jurisdictions and therefore increase complexity, and adapt their behavior to counter or neutralize law enforcement initiatives.[16]

By the first decade of the twenty-first century, the northern tier countries of Central America had three of the five highest homicide rates in the world, far higher than it was during the war. El Salvador, Guatemala, and Honduras measured consistently among the five highest murder rates globally, ranging from 50 to 71 homicides per 100,000 citizens. This compares to about 5 murders per 100,000 in the United States and 1.7 in Canada.

The murder rate for people aged 15 to 24 in El Salvador specifically was an unbelievable 94 per 100,000—the highest in the world.[17]

By 2003, the internal structures of the gangs consolidated with the top tier leaders often in the United States. Many stayed there because they were less likely to be imprisoned as the governments in Central America, desperate for a solution, began rounding up gang members, often identified by their tattoos. This policy of *mano dura* (heavy hand) against the gangs initially brought some relief, but also allowed the gang members to take over prison facilities and consolidate their communications and logistics networks.[18]

The emerging gang structure relied on *clicas* (cliques), or local neighborhood groups, under the command of a *palabrero*, who is responsible for 20 to 30 *clicas*. Above him is a *ranflero*—a leader of multiple *palabreros*, chosen by geographic area. The *ranflero* is generally in prison, but his word is law. Above the *ranfleros* are the *jefes nacionales*, a small group of national leaders who have the ultimate authority on issues that affect the entire structure. Within this structure, local gang leaders have considerable autonomy in deciding which criminal activities to engage in as a clique, how to distribute criminal proceeds, and which nongang TCOs to work with.[19]

THE TRANSITION

Over time, the gangs, particularly MS-13, grew in size and strength, operating with virtual impunity in much of El Salvador and maintaining a significant presence in Honduras and Guatemala. According to a 2011 report by the National Police antigang unit in El Salvador, by the end of 2010, the MS-13 and Calle 18 gangs had some 27,500 members just in El Salvador, 9,200 of whom were in prison.[20] As a useful point of comparison, the guerrilla group Farabundo Martí National Liberation Front (FMLN) had at its peak in 1983, some 9,000 to 12,000 combatants, and remained a formidable enough force to negotiate an end to the war without surrendering.

Regional UN officials and other experts estimate the number is at least as great in Honduras, and likely more in Guatemala. This means the gangs have at least some 80,000 members whose primary loyalty is to the gangs rather than any state, operating in a territory the size of three small states in the United States.[21]

A significant turning point for the gangs, particularly the MS-13, which tends to be more disciplined, larger, and cohesive than the Calle 18 groups, was the declaration of war against the Mexican cartels by Mexican president Felipe Calderón. As the violence and pressure on the Mexican DTOs began to take its toll, the two largest organizations, the Sinaloa Cartel and Los Zetas, began to open new inroads into Central America, which went beyond simply using gang members as their foot soldiers.

This coincided with the reemergence of Central America as a major transshipment corridor—a result of U.S. and Caribbean counternarcotics measures that focused on eliminating such trade from traditional sea routes—with up to 90 percent of the cocaine reaching the United States passing through Central America and Mexico.[22] As the pressure on the Mexican cartels grew inside Mexico, and the groups themselves engaged in fierce intracartel warfare, control of the Central American routes became increasingly important to the organizations that had the capacity to project themselves into the area.

Given this shift, the strength of the existing gangs in the region had to be factored in and dealt with. The gangs were simply too big to ignore and too useful as a potential workforce not to take into account. The question for the gangs, according to MS-13 members, was whether they would work for the cartels, try to fight off the encroachment of the cartels, or look for another type of arrangement with them.

Until about 2008, the primary function of the gangs had been to protect cocaine shipments produced by Colombian cartels. The loads were shipped by these groups to Central America from Ecuador, Colombia, and Venezuela through a variety of methods. Once the loads reached Central America, they were largely turned over to the Mexican organizations and had to be moved by land from their point of entry across the Mexican border, through Mexico, and, finally, into the United States.

Often the Mexican drug traffickers accepted the handover of cocaine in El Salvador and then moved the product north through Guatemala to Mexico and northward. This led to the development of specialized drug transport networks led by *transportistas*, or smuggling specialists, who were often protected or escorted by gangs such as MS-13. They were often given a small percentage of the cocaine they helped to protect.[23]

This payment, in kind rather than in cash, had become a major factor in the escalating violence. Once the gangs received cocaine, they had to create a local market to absorb it in order to earn cash. This *narco menudeo*, or small scale retail of cocaine and crack, set off an ongoing battle among different gangs for control over neighborhoods and street corners where the drugs could be sold, leading to widespread bloodshed. A similar dynamic is responsible for much of the violence in other high-risk areas such as Ciudad Juárez in Mexico, where local gangs also fight for control of local distribution.[24] As the gangs' income from working more closely with TCOs increased, so did the type of weapons they could buy and the ruthlessness with which they could attack.

A consequence of this newfound power was the protection money or "taxes" demanded by the gangs from local businesses and services. For example, in El Salvador, MS-13 began to force bus owners to pay increasingly onerous taxes on public transportation networks, which were lucrative in part because the owners received extensive government subsidies. As gang territory grew, so did the amount that bus owners had to pay in order to move their vehicles across the city. Finally, bus owners decided to join together not to pay taxes—a direct challenge to gang authority.[25]

In June 2010, in a chilling display, the gangs attacked two crowded buses as they moved through the center of San Salvador. One of the buses was sprayed with automatic weapons fire, while the other was doused with gasoline and set on fire with all the passengers inside, including a four-month-old baby. Police said the violence was aimed at bus drivers who refused to pay the protection money to the gang members who controlled the territory along the bus routes.[26] Some press versions attributed the attack to a revenge killing among gangs, but police investigators discounted that version.[27] The incident prompted El Salvador's president, Mauricio Funes, to brand the attacks "acts of terrorism," and provided the necessary impetus for the National Assembly to overwhelmingly pass a tough new law designating membership in a gang, regardless of individual activity, a crime punishable by jail time. President Funes also dispatched 1,000 army troops to support the police in combating gang activity, in addition to the 5,000 troops already deployed.[28]

TOWARD A STRONGER ALLIANCE

Even with the influx of more cocaine, the growing presence of the Mexican cartels, and the possibility of greater financial gain, the gangs had no clear policy of how or when to move into more active roles.

Respective gang factions made different decisions at different times about how to relate to the Mexican organizations as the process went forward. There was no centralized decision making; different cliques and different groups of cliques made independent decisions on how to build that relationship. This has made it hard to make broad statements about the relationships between the gangs and TCOs, which is unlikely to change in the near future, as the relative strength among the groups shift, alliances are tested, and the political situation evolves across the region.

However, there are identifiable trends. The main shift in the past two years has been the clear evidence that the gangs, rather than just killing rival gang members and other local enemies, are increasingly acting as armed groups hired by the cartels as hit men and muscle, a difference from their previous roles as mere foot soldiers.

There is also growing evidence that the gangs, rather than limiting themselves to their traditional role of small-scale retailers in poor local neighborhoods, are now moving multikilo loads of cocaine, which has raised their income to even higher levels. It is likely that this is the result of their greater role in cartel security and protection, leading to higher payments of cocaine for their services.

The relationships also vary from country to country. In Guatemala, the relationship, where there is one, is with the Zetas. In El Salvador, some gangs are forming alliances with major national organizations such as Los Perrones in the eastern region or El Cartel de Texis in the north central and western regions. In Honduras, the primary relationships are with the Sinaloa cartel, which is the predominant group that controls trafficking operations around San Pedro Sula and the landing strips along the Atlantic coast.[29]

This does not mean there haven't been conflicts. In 2010, a clique of the MS-13 group that extorted many illegal immigrants hopping the famous train that runs from southern Mexico to the U.S. border found the Zetas trying to push them out of business. A bloody war ensued for several months, with multiple dead on both sides. In the end, a sort of truce was agreed to, with MS-13 taxing the southern part of the route and the Zetas taxing the northern sector.

"We can't let ourselves be run off by anyone in our territory," said one gang member with direct knowledge of the events. "We can work with anyone, but we won't work for anyone. That was what the fight was about."[30]

By 2010, President Funes acknowledged this transformation in alliances, saying:

> At the beginning, the gangs were just a group of rebel youngsters. As time moved on, the gangs became killers for hire. Now the situation is that the gangs have become part of the whole thing. They control territory and they are disputing territory with the drug traffickers. Why? Because they need to finance their way of life: basically, getting arms.[31]

Perhaps the most dangerous trend is the emergence of training camps, with gang members being trained by the larger TCOs. For example, MS-13 cliques such as Fulton Locos Salvatruchas (FLS), the most violent of the identified gang cliques, operates in close conjunction with the Cartel de

Texis in El Salvador, and has reportedly received training from Los Zetas at camps in Petén, Guatemala, near the Mexican border.[32]

MS-13 members in San Salvador say that there are also mobile training camps set up by Los Zetas in the volcanoes outside San Salvador, in hard to reach areas where the FMLN once had strongholds. According to these sources, some of those trained have been hired by the Mexicans to work in Mexico for a basic salary of $400 for their services. In some cases, the money is paid to the MS-13 member's clique, rather than to the member himself. Those interviewed were reluctant to quantify the number of people who have been trained or had been hired by Los Zetas, saying only that "it has not been so many."[33]

There are increasing indications that such training and these closer relationships are making the Central American gangs better armed and better trained, and pushing them to operate on behalf of TCOs rather than just their own gangs. For example, based on police intelligence reports, *InSightCrime*, a leading website tracking organized crime in Latin America, reported that an MS-13 leader warned authorities in January 2010 of a potential offensive. The report said that:

> The leader did not specify what he meant but authorities are linking this threat, made last year, with a February 6 massacre in Tonacatepeque, just north of San Salvador in which masked men armed with M-16 semi-automatics and 9 mm pistols shot and killed six people in a restaurant. The massacre came a day after seven people were killed in a similar manner in Suchitoto, just northeast of Tonacatepeque. Another police intelligence report obtained by InSight said one of the victims in the Tonacatepeque massacre was linked to a drug trafficking organization along the border with Guatemala, along the same corridor police suspect the Zetas may be aiming to control.[34]

CONCLUSIONS

Within the context of their growing economic power and armed strength, the March 2012 truce between the gangs in El Salvador and the concessions granted by Salvadoran government-sanctioned negotiators points to several new realities.[35] While the truce has not been adopted in other countries outside of El Salvador, gang leaders in Honduras and Guatemala have said they are considering it. On studying the Salvadoran model, it appears that these trends may have regional applicability. The first major shift is that the gangs now have become aware of the potential to exercise real political influence based on their territorial control, armed power, and access to increasing resources. Since the truce was signed, national gang leaders have issued several orders designed to improve the image of the groups in the neighborhoods where they live, as well as on a broader scale.

> SINCE THE TRUCE WAS SIGNED, THE NUMBER OF HOMICIDES HAS DECREASED MARKEDLY, ALTHOUGH NOT AS STEEPLY AS THE GOVERNMENT CLAIMS.

These include pledges to stop recruiting elementary school children into their ranks, halting the practice of extorting local merchants and food vendors in their neighborhoods, and reducing the taxes collected from public transportation buses. Since the truce was signed, the number of homicides has decreased markedly, although not as steeply as the government claims.[36] Rather than leaving the bodies of homicide victims on the streets as a message to their enemies, gang members now bury the bodies in clandestine cemeteries.[37]

While it is unclear how this evolving political role will manifest itself outside of negotiations with the government on specific gang-related issues, gang leaders say they have already been approached by leaders of different political parties offering support for favorable laws in exchange for the votes of those in gang-controlled territories.[38] This will only make the gangs even more attractive to the TCOs that are already engaged in extensive political and judicial corruption in the region.

The second major shift is that the truce will likely allow the gangs a respite from intergang fighting and a chance to consolidate their relationships with Mexican drug cartels and other TCOs from a position of increased strength.

As noted, MS-13 members, at least, have resisted working for the Mexicans and view themselves as strong enough to be partners rather than employees. Given the significant military force the Mexican cartels would have to project into unfamiliar and unfriendly territory in order to win a military struggle, they have so far not tried to take over territory. This is in contrast to Guatemala where Los Zetas, operating across a porous border with Mexico, controls considerable territory and transit routes.[39]

If the rivalry between the two gangs eases not just in El Salvador, but across the region, MS-13 and Calle 18 will each have neutralized their most lethal enemy. This will allow them time and resources to consolidate their territorial control and enter into more permanent alliances with TCOs.

One reason why this consolidation with the DTOs has not yet taken place, according to regional intelligence officials in El Salvador and Mexico, is that the Mexican cartels and other TCOs find the gang members to be too undisciplined and volatile in their wars with each other to be reliable partners in the drug trade. As this changes, a main obstacle to a more cohesive relationship with the Mexican organizations will be removed.

These two shifts have made gangs an increasingly important national security priority for Central America, Mexico, and the United States.[40] The integration of these gangs, with their territorial control and growing political power, within the TCOs is already wreaking havoc on the region, its fragile institutions, and democratic processes.

Since their inception, gangs in the region have shown a high level of adaptability, coherence, creativity, and resilience. These traits have been combined with their capacity for ruthless violence, which has grown as their ties to the TCOs have deepened and their resource base has been enhanced. Given the visible signs that gangs and TCOs have developed closer tactical ties that continue to evolve and grow, it is probable that a more strategic alliance will be formed between the groups. Both sides stand to benefit: the gangs gain enhanced earnings, better weapons, and political sway; the TCOs receive enhanced protection and impunity, as well as improved transportation networks. The potential synergy presented by a strategic alliance could be enormously attractive to all sides.

These developments will continue to be an enormous challenge to the governments of the region, who so far have failed to develop any strategy—unilateral or multilateral—to blunt either the growth of the gangs or the power and influence of TCOs. With endemic corruption, a dearth of resources, and few functioning institutions, the next level of alliance between the gangs and TCOs could be catastrophic for the region and pose significant security challenges for the United States and its efforts to work with Mexico to slow the flow of cocaine northward.

NOTES

1. Douglas Farah, "The Transformation of El Salvador's Gangs into Political Actors" (Center for Strategic and International Studies (CSIS), Washington, DC: 22 June 2012). For a brief look at that element see http://csis.org/publication/transformation-el-salvadors-gangs-political-actors.

2. Indira A.R. Lakshmanan, "Cocaine's New Route: Traffickers Turn to Guatemala," *Boston Globe*, 30 November 2005. For a broader historic overview, see Peter J. Meyer and Clare Ribando Seelke, "Central America Regional Security Initiative: Background and Policy Issues for Congress," (Congressional Research Service, 21 February 2012), 7–9.

3. For more details on the truce and its origins, see Douglas Farah, "The Transformation of El Salvador's Gangs into Political Actors," (Center for

Strategic and International Studies (CSIS), Washington DC: 21 June 2012), http://csis.org/files/publication/120621_Farah_Gangs_HemFocus.pdf.

4. Moisés Naim, *Illicit: How Smugglers, Traffickers and Copycats are Hijacking the Global Economy* (New York: Random House, 2005), 33.

5. John P. Sullivan, "Gangs, Hooligans and Anarchists—The Vanguard of Netwar on the Streets" in *Networks and Netwars: The Future of Terror, Crime and Militancy*, ed. John Arquilla and David Rondfelt (Santa Monica: Rand Corporation, 2001), 99–127.

6. Max. G. Manwaring, "Street Gangs: The New Urban Insurgency" (report, Strategic Studies Institute, U.S. Army War College: March 2005), http://www.strategicstudiesinstitute.army.mil/pubs/display.cfm?pubID=597.

7. For a good overview of the steps taken, see Ana Arana "How Street Gangs Took Central America," *Foreign Affairs* 84, no. 3 (May/June 2005), 98–110.

8. Ibid., 100.

9. Author extrapolation of numbers provided by the Congressional Research Service for those years can be found in the following publication: Clare Ribando Seelke, "Gangs in Central America" (report, Congressional Research Service, 3 January 2011), 9, http://www.fas.org/sgp/crs/row/RL34112.pdf.

10. From the late 1970s until the early 1990s Central America was wracked by a series of internal conflicts and proxy wars that were part of the Cold War. The 1979 triumph of the Sandinista revolution in Nicaragua, backed by the Soviet Union and Cuba, helped fuel the nascent Marxist-led Farabundo Martí National Liberation Front (*Frente Farabundo Martí para la Liberación Nacional* [FMLN]) insurgency in neighboring El Salvador and Guatemala. In response, the United States backed the governments of El Salvador and Guatemala and funded the Contra rebels based in Honduras to fight the Sandinista government. All three conflicts ended in negotiated settlements in the early 1990s. The Nicaraguan conflict ended with the elections of 1990 with the defeat of the Sandinistas. The Salvadoran conflict ended in a peace accord in 1992 and the Guatemalan conflict ended in 1994. For an overview of the conflicts see Clifford Krauss, *Inside Central America: Its People, Politics and History* (New York: Summit Books, 1991, 1992).

11. Arana, 99.

12. As a correspondent at the *Washington Post*, I was able to document this phenomenon in 1995, where U.S.-trained members of elite military units and Cuban-trained members of elite guerrilla units joined together to run one of the largest MS-13 gangs at the time. See Douglas Farah and Tod Robberson, "U.S.-Style Gangs in El Salvador Build Free Trade in Crime," *Washington Post*, 28 August 1995.

13. The investigation was carried out by a special commission formed in 1992, composed of the nation's human rights ombudsman, a representative of the UN Secretary General, and two representatives of the Salvadoran government. The commission was formed by a political agreement among all the major parties due to a resurgence in political violence after the signing of the historic peace accords. See "Informe del Grupo Conjunto Para la Investigación de Grupos Armados Ilegales con Motivación Política en El Salvador," (Report of the Joint Investigative Group on Illegal Armed Groups and their Political Roots, El Salvador: 28 July 1994), http://www.uca.edu.sv/publica/idhuca/grupo.html.

14. Farah and Robberson, 1995; and author interview with gang members.

15. Jeffrey S. Passel, "Estimates of the Size and Characteristics of the Undocumented Population" (Pew Hispanic Research Center), 21 March 2005, 2; Author interviews with gang members.

16. Phil Williams, "Transnational Criminal Networks" in *Networks and Netwars: The Future of Terror, Crime and Militancy*, ed. John Arquilla and David Rondfelt (Santa Monica: Rand Corporation, 2001), 78.

17. There are multiple studies on the number of homicides in the region, which vary slightly in the exact numbers but arrive at the same general number. These studies show the homicide rate in El Salvador almost doubling from about 37 per 100,000 in 2004 to about 71 per 100,000 in 2009. For official National Police statistics see: "Número de Victimas y Tasas de Homicidios Dolosos en El Salvador (1999–2006)," Observatorio Centroamericano Sobre Violencia, 3 September 2010. Also see: Edith Portillo, "Gestión de Saca Acumula 16 mil homicidios," El Faro, 29 December 2008; and "Crime and Instability: Case Studies of Transnational Threats," UN Office of Drugs and Crime, United Nations, February 2010. The figure on homicides among young people was

taken from: Canwest News Service, "Latin America Has the Highest Homicide Rate for Young Adults in the World," 26 November 2008.

18. For a more complete look at the impact of the *mano dura* policies see Seelke, 9.

19. Author interviews with gang members and Policía Nacional.

20. Policía Nacional de El Salvador, "Las Estructuras de las Pandillas MS13 y 18 en El Salvador," (The Structures of the MS13 and 18 in El Salvador), September 2011, in possession of the author. This was the most comprehensive study on gangs ever conducted in El Salvador and mapped the structures by city block in major cities and towns. Other estimates by the FBI and UNODC of the gang size are smaller. See http://www.fbi.gov/news/stories/2006/april/burrus041906 and http://www.start. umd.edu/start/data_collections/tops/terrorist_organization_profile.asp?id=228.

21. Author interviews with INTERPOL officials and UN officials in El Salvador, Guatemala, and Mexico City in 2011 and 2012.

22. Peter J. Meyer and Clare Ribando Seelke, "Central America Regional Security Initiative: Background and Policy Issues for Congress," Congressional Research Service, 21 February 2012, 8.

23. Farah and Robberson; Steven Dudley, "Central America's 'Transportistas,'" *InSight: Organized Crime in the Americas*, 21 November 2010, http://insightcrime. org/investigations/insight-exclusives/item/255-insight-brief-central-americas-transportistas.

24. Author interviews with Mexican and U.S. law enforcement and civil society organizations in Ciudad Juarez and El Paso, TX, March 2011.

25. Author interviews with MS-13 members and Salvadoran law enforcement officials, July 2010.

26. Alex Renderos, "16 Killed in Salvador Bus Attacks," *Los Angeles Times*, 21 June 2010.

27. Author interviews with MS-13 members and Salvadoran law enforcement officials, July 2010.

28. EFE News Agency, "Salvadoran Signs Tough Anti-Gang Measure Into Law," 10 September 2010.

29. For the best look at the multiple variations in the types of relationships that have developed, see Steven Dudley "Inside: Maras' Connections to Criminal Syndicates Growing," *InSightCrime*, 22 January 2011, http://www.insightcrime. org/investigations/maras-connections-to-criminal-syndicates-growing; Author interviews with regional Honduran security officials in May 2012.

30. Interview with member of the MS-13 gang involved in the conflict and verified by Central American law enforcement officials.

31. Los Angeles Times Staff Report, "Salvadoran Leader Speaks of Criminal Gangs' Links to Drug Cartels," *Los Angeles Times*, 11 September 2010, http://articles. latimes.com/2010/sep/ll/world/la-fg-salvador-funes-20100911.

32. Elyssa Pachico, "Salvador Drug Cartel Targeted in Rare Arrest," *InSightCrime*, 28 May 2012, http://www.insightcrime.org/news-briefs/ secretive-el-savador-drug-cartel-targeted-in-rare-arrest; Dudley, "Inside: Maras Connections to Criminal Syndicates Growing," *InSightCrime*, 22 January 2011, http://www.insightcrime.org/investigations/maras-connections-to-criminal-syndicates-growing.

33. Interview with MS-13 gang members in San Salvador, May 2012.

34. Dudley, 2011.

35. Douglas Farah, "The Transformation of El Salvador's Gangs into Political Actors," (report, CSIS, 21 June 2012), http://csis.org/files/publication/120621_Farah_Gangs_ HemFocus.pdf; Rachael Schwartz, "El Salvador's Gang Truce Raises Troubling Questions for the Region," *World Politics Review*, 11 May 2012, http://www.worldpoliticsreview. com/articles/11941/el-salvador-gang-truce-raises-troubling-questions-for-region.

36. Latin American Herald Tribune, "Funes: Gang Truce Cut Murders 52% in El Salvador Since March," 13 September 2012, http://www.laht.com/article.asp? CategoryId=23558&ArticleId=539085. See Geoffrey Ramsey "A Closer Look at El Salvador's Homicide Stats," *InsightCrime*, September 6, 2012, http://www.in-sightcrime.org/news-analysis/a-closer-look-at-el-salvadors-homicide-stats?utm_ content=dfarah%40mac.com&utm_source=VerticalResponse&utm_medium =Email&utm_term=A%20Closer%20Look%20at%20El%20Salvador%26% 2339%3Bs%20Homicide%20Stats&utm_campaign=Weekly%20InSight% 3A%20%22El%20Coss%22%20Captured%2C%20Questions%20for%20 Colombia%27s%20Peace%20Processcontent.

37. Douglas Farah, "The Transformation of El Salvador's Gangs into Political Actors," (report, CSIS, 21 June 2012), http://csis.org/files/publication/120621_ Farah_Gangs_HemFocus.pdf 2; Rachael Schwartz, "El Salvador's Gang Truce

Raises Troubling Questions for the Region," *World Politics Review*, 11 May 2012, http://www.worldpoliticsreview.com/articles/11941/el-salvador-gang-truce-raises-troubling-questions-for-region.

38. Interview with MS-13 gang members in San Salvador, June 2012.

39. "Zetas Guatemala," *InsightCrime*, 22 August 2012, http://www.insightcrime.org/component/k2/item/628-zetas.

40. The most recent FBI National Gang Assessment states that, "Gangs are expanding, evolving and posing an increasing threat to U.S. communities nationwide. Many gangs are sophisticated criminal networks with members who are violent, distribute wholesale quantities of drugs, and develop and maintain close working relationships with members and associates of transnational criminal/drug trafficking organizations. Gangs are becoming more violent while engaging in less typical and lower-risk crime, such as prostitution and white-collar crime. Gangs are more adaptable, organized, sophisticated, and opportunistic, exploiting new and advanced technology as a means to recruit, communicate discretely, target their rivals, and perpetuate their criminal activity." See National Gang Intelligence Center, "FBI National Gang Threat Assessment: Emerging Trends," (February 2012).

CENTRAL AMERICAN GANG VIOLENCE IN 2019

"EFFORTS AT REFORM"

By Robert Kirkland and Duncan Breda

The level of gang violence in Central America continues to be a humanitarian crisis. Gang violence is centered in El Salvador, Guatemala, and Honduras and is fueled and supported by the drug trade into the United States. The aim of this article is to summarize the gang violence situation in these three Central American countries and provide a prediction as to the possibility of decreased violence in the future.

EL SALVADOR

As of 2017, El Salvador continued to have the worst violence in Central America. Mara Salvatrucha, known colloquially as "MS-13," and Barrio 18, or "18th Street Gang," have given this small nation the highest murder rate in the Western Hemisphere. The level of violence and bloodshed has caused the government to scramble to find ways to stop the killing from continuing in their streets.

Experts estimate that 70,000 people in the country of six million belong to gangs, with at least a half million more involved in the economic activities of the gangs. In many of the villages and cities of the country, the gangs have taken complete control, using checkpoints to monitor resident movement in and out of their towns.

The Salvadoran government continued to actively fight the gangs in their strongholds, which resulted in an uptick in violence in 2016—both from gang and government forces. According to the *Washington Post*, soldiers and police were being linked to human rights abuses and assassinations. The violence led to a mass exodus of El Salvador's population as they fled the violence. It is estimated that 9,000 Salvadorans per month attempted to travel to the United States to escape the violence.

Particularly in the past year, the Salvadoran military has come into great conflict with gangs and drug traffickers, reaching a peak after Salvadoran President Sanchez Ceren declared war on them in April 2016. This has resulted in open warfare. There are 10,400 soldiers on the streets of El Salvador now, with the Sanchez Ceren government unleashing a 1,000-strong special reaction force (FERES), including 600 soldiers. This has caused violence to increase. El Salvador remains the most violent country outside a recognized war zone.

Nevertheless, compared to the earlier efforts, some government efforts seem to hold out hope for a better outcome. The changes revolve around attempting to control the gangs from the prisons. Salvadoran prisons are overcrowded and controlled by the gangs, with little interference from the wardens and guards. The leaders of the gangs have been able to operate from behind bars using smuggled cell phones and continue to orchestrate drug trafficking, extortion, murders, and kidnappings. The leaders of these gangs are essentially left to run their operations from prison untouched.

By late 2018 and into 2019, cracking down on the corruption and paraphernalia within their prison system has enabled the Salvadoran government to slowly cut off the gangs' ability to communicate with their imprisoned leaders. This has allowed the government to begin to gain the upper hand on the gangs.

In sum, in El Salvador, the police have been able to gain ground against the gangs, and while some see this as a victory, many in the population still see law enforcement as the country's most dangerous threat, given police brutality against civilians in combating the gangs. The violence in El Salvador has become so bad that it is hard to determine who, if anyone, is looking out for the best interests of the population.

HONDURAS

Honduras, like El Salvador, has seen more than its fair share of violence. Since 2008, it too has been involved in a war on gangs that has turned this Central American country into a war zone. At one point, Honduras was one of the top three murder capitals in the world (per capita). However, multiple sources are reporting that the Honduran government may have begun to turn the tide at the end of 2016. Violence has begun to decrease, mainly due to the assistance that Honduras is receiving from the United States.

Honduras, compared to El Salvador and Guatemala, has enjoyed an exceedingly close relationship with the United States. Soto Cano Air Base (commonly known as Palmerola Air Base) is home to more than a thousand US service members who work with the Hondurans on antidrug and antigang efforts. The Honduran government decided to adopt the gang-reduction and -prevention strategy that proved effective in Boston and Los Angeles in the 1990s. It involved concentrating efforts on the most violent hot spots. The Honduran police used three test locations. In these locations, there are 46 neighborhood outreach centers that provide mentors and vocational training, giving their citizens the skills to find good jobs, which will help to prevent them from joining the gangs.

The United States has also provided aid to the Honduran government to help witnesses testify against the gangs. This is a difficult task, given that gangs have often threatened those who testify against them with death. Thus, it takes a great deal of government assistance and pledges of protection to get witnesses to come forward. According to Honduran authorities, it takes four to 15 visits (of police or government officials) to persuade a witness to testify. This means that takes a lot of work, money, and time just to be able to bring these witnesses to court to testify against these gangs.

These reforms were starting to show progress as we moved to 2017. However, the increased incarceration of gang members put strains on their prison system, though it helped hold the country's murderers accountable. Before, Honduran gang violence was unchecked. Now, gang members are being tried and punished for crimes at a greater rate. This has proven expensive but worth the cost.

What's concerning about Honduras in 2019 is that MS-13 seems to be the key transportation group for Mexican drug cartels in the northern part of Honduras, replacing Mafia families who have controlled the drug trade for years. Given this, there is a strong possibility that there will be an increase in the power of MS-13 in northern Honduran cities such as San Pedro Sula, which could pose problems for the government.

Honduras, with the help of the United States, has cut its murder rate nearly in half in 2019. It is possible that if El Salvador and Guatemala were to implement these processes as well, they would be able to see the same positive results. The issue with using the Honduran model is that it is expensive and requires the help of a country with the resources of the United States. There also must be the political will to carry out these reforms. The jury is still out as to whether El Salvador or Guatemala will adopt these strategies that have proven so successful in Honduras.

GUATEMALA

Finally, Guatemala has perhaps been impacted the most by the refugee crisis caused by those fleeing gang violence. With Guatemala's proximity to El Salvador and Honduras and its position as a way station to the United States, many refugees, given the difficulty of travel in Mexico and crossing the border to the United States, have decided to stop and stay in Guatemala rather than continue. This decision has strained Guatemalan support structures as the country deals with tens of thousands of refugees.

What many of these refugees find upon arrival in Guatemala is that gangs hold as much sway in Guatemala as they do in Honduras and El Salvador. The gangs have exploited these vulnerable refugees by extorting or kidnapping them. Guatemalan gangs have also tortured and killed refugees on behalf of gang members in Honduras and El Salvador. Thus, refugees often find they are not safe from the gangs even though they have left their home country.

Given the crisis in Guatemala, there is less reason for optimism regarding refugees and the strains on the Guatemalan support structure. Nevertheless, Guatemala continues to receive substantial aid from the United States to help resettle refugees as well as to reform the police and military to combat the gangs. This aid is showing progress, but not as much as in El Salvador or Honduras.

CONCLUSION

By the end of 2017, the level of gang violence had become so prevalent that many were considering it a humanitarian crisis. However, if Honduras and El Salvador are any indicator, with reasoned reform efforts, the violence may be controllable. It is not something that will be immediate, but it may be accomplished over time. The people of the region will need to have a great deal of resolve and patience to be successful.

five

This article explores the under-studied topic of transnational generational gangs and the major factors leading them to grow into powerful, politically motivated insurgencies. While insurgent movements have been recognized as the most widespread forms of warfare since the early nineteenth century, states and their enforcement entities still have yet to completely and effectively tailor their responses to such issues. After a brief introduction to generational gangs and insurgencies), the evolution of gangs and the greater implications of this issue will be outlined. The effects of gang evolution and insurgency development due to globalization, the democratization of technology, and culture will be discussed in the "Implications" section. Also, an explanation of why this is pertinent to the United States, specifically Latin American and Caribbean relations, is provided.

GENERATIONAL GANGS AND INSURGENCY

THE NEW BATTLEFRONT FOR LAW ENFORCEMENT OFFICERS

By José de Arimatéia da Cruz, Taylor Alvarez and James Madison Marye

INTRODUCTION

Insurgency is the most widespread form of warfare today. Indeed though military establishments persist in regarding it as "irregular" or "unconventional," guerrilla war has been the commonest of conflicts throughout history, occurring in one variety or another in almost all known societies. In the modern era, the Correlates of War Project, a scholarly database maintained since 1963, identifies 464 wars that occurred between 1816 and the end of the twentieth century, of which only 79 (17 percent) were "conventional" interstate conflicts between the regular armed forces of nation-states, while 385 (just under 83 percent of recorded conflicts) were civil wars or insurgencies. (Kilcullen, 2010, pp. ix–x)

José de Arimatéia da Cruz, PhD, Taylor Alvarez and James Madison Marye, "Generational Gangs and Insurgency: The New Battlefront for Law Enforcement Officers," Law Enforcement Executive Forum, pp. 38-47. Copyright © 2016 by I.L.E.T.S.B. Executive Institute. Reprinted with permission.

Despite these undeniable statistics about the prevalence of insurgencies and asymmetrical conflict throughout history, research and responsive action has yet to completely adapt as needed to counter it. As Lieutenant Walter Herd (2002) acknowledged in his research: "Frequently organizations are *forced* to change *after* they find themselves no longer relevant in an ever-changing environment" (p. 1). As various parts of the world continually fall victim to insurgent movements and gang activity—the most notable currently being ISIS and cartels along the U.S-Mexican border—increasingly, more states are having to face the reality of unconventional conflict. It is clear that sheer force, like that boasted by the U.S. Armed Forces, is no longer substantial enough on its own to quell dissent and violence (U.S. Government, 2012).

Renken (2013) notes that gangs inherently arise from a desire for money—what is considered *power*. Globalization and the democratization of technology allow insurgents and organized crime organizations, as well as everyday citizens, to interact and wield a digital platform almost effortlessly. As the global economy continues to grow, realization of the parallel political and social gains are likely to follow as does the desire for further success (Sullivan, 2008). Sullivan (2008) explains that civil unrest can give way to political and violent uprising as digital devices and a shared sense of identity or discontent organize massive amounts of people. As a result, countermeasures to these asymmetrical concerns must take into account the origins and forces driving organized crime, terrorism, and insurgency. Understanding gangs—and as they continue to grow in size and ambition, insurgencies—as well as how culture, political and social climate, and technology interact with these increasingly pertinent concerns, is necessary to better combat them (Department of the Army, 2014, pp. 1.1–5.7).

WHY ANALYZE GANG NETWORKS?

Analyzing the future of conflict is nothing new: Insurgencies and civil war have been the prevailing conflict for the last 200 years. With the evolution of gangs as the focus of this analysis, the intent is to demonstrate how gangs can manifest. Gangs arise from a sense of localized turf-criminality before growing into a realized regional threat. Gangs boast regional destabilization and threaten the stability of governing institutions. Eventually, they emerge as a globally networked insurgency effectively usurping established political regimes and institutions via political actions and violence.

In Stephen Metz's (1993) *The Future of Insurgency*, he describes two types of insurgencies: (1) *spiritual* and (2) *commercial*. *Spiritual insurgencies*, the descendents of Cold War-driven *revolutionary insurgencies*, are driven by problems with globalization and modernization, the search for meaning, or the pursuit of justice against injustices—whether those injustices are real or perceived. Spiritual insurgencies have come to replace revolutionary insurgencies fostered and sponsored by Marxist ideology due to a lack of support and funding, which has dried up in the wake of the collapse of the Soviet Union (Metz, 1993).

Commercial insurgencies are driven less by desire for justice than wealth—a widespread perception of Western popular culture, which equates wealth to personal meaning, and power (Metz, 1993). Metz (1993) states that people who are frustrated to the point of violence, but lacking the ability to directly challenge the institutions responsible, will inevitably resort to insurgency as the only form of political violence that can usurp the established powers that be. Metz further posits that the fall of the USSR has exacerbated the problem of insurgencies by creating a vacuum of power in regions with typically weak centralized governing institutions that now lack the backing power of a world *superpower* to aid in their being (remaining) the primary governing institution.

Finally, Metz (1993) explains how the prevalence of one type of insurgency over the other will vary:

[T]he dominance of one of these two forms will vary from region to region. Latin America is likely to suffer more from continued and expanded commercial insurgency than from spiritual. Sub-Saharan Africa will be particularly prone to insurgency. . . . The likelihood of spiritual insurgency is also high in the Middle East (including Arab North Africa).

Max G. Manwaring (2005), former Professor of Military Strategy in the Strategic Studies Institute (SSI) of the U.S. Army War College (USAWC), in his study of gangs as a form of insurgency, identifies the "universal" complexities of gang violence and its effect on society. Manwaring identifies three "levels of analysis": (1) gangs generate serious domestic and regional instability that range from personal violence to insurgency and can ultimately lead to state failure; (2) gangs exacerbate civil-military relations and police-military relation problems, and they can further reduce effectiveness of civil-military ability to control the national territory and maintain the order of law; and (3) gangs in their support of transnational criminal organizations, insurgents, warlords, and drug barons all help to erode the legitimacy and effective sovereignty of states and their institutions. Manwaring summarizes the concept of *third generation gangs* in the following way: "Insurgents and third generation gangs are engaged in a highly complex political act—political war."

PARAMETERS OF ANALYSIS

For the analysis of gang evolution, the main focus will be placed on how gang criminality drives political violence and insurgency. The theoretical approach set forward by John P. Sullivan (1997) will be adopted. According to Sullivan, gangs fall under one of three generational evolutions: *first generation, second generation,* and *third generation* (pp. 95–108). Within each of these generational evolutions is an inherent capacity, both politically and upon a spectrum of violence and criminality, for each generation to achieve its goals.

General Evolution of Gangs

First generation gangs or *turf gangs* (also referred to as "turf warriors" by Sullivan, 1997) are gangs that are localized and primarily "turf" oriented in that they are seeking to maintain the primary influence over a designated area; they are highly decentralized in their command and control structure. Turf gangs typically engage in inter-gang rivalries and take advantage of opportunistic criminal activities more so than a more sophisticated outlook in committing criminal acts for financial gain. Due to being highly localized in territory and possessing a decentralized and unsophisticated hierarchy, turf gangs are severely limited in political scope. Sullivan (1997) classifies turf gangs as "proto-net warriors" (p. 96, Table 1). *Proto-net warriors* are the infancy of *NetWar* participants; first generation gangs are not sophisticated or in a secure enough position to utilize technology in a manner that will centralize their command and control hierarchy or unify the organization around a singular or cohesive political aim.

Second generation gangs or, as they are better known, *cartels* are inherently more sophisticated than their first generation predecessors. According to Sullivan (1997), cartels are drug-centric, entrepreneurial enterprises that are more concerned in cornering and protecting drug markets than controlling turf. Cartels tend to have a limited political scope and capability; they generally focus on the market of which they are a part. Cartels are continually becoming multi-state oriented; they embrace the exercise of violence in what Sullivan describes as quasi-terrorism in order to command influence and provide protection for the cartel's market. Sullivan describes cartels as "emerging net warriors" (p. 99).

As *emerging net warriors*, the cartels are the median of violence, internationalization, and sophistication (Sullivan, 1997, pp. 95–108). These cartels are becoming increasingly connected—*networked*—and are also becoming increasingly sophisticated via technology and what David Kilcullen (2010) calls the "democratization of technology," meaning that technology once reserved for the state and the extremely wealthy has over time, and at an increasingly accelerated pace, become cheaper and more easily purchased by individuals who previously could not afford or have the capability of using such technologies. This increased connectedness makes the cartels' grip on (1) their preferred market, (2) centralization of command and control structure, and (3) cohesively and effectively enacting political violence and/ or unifying around a unified political goal much easier and efficient.

Lastly, *third generation gangs* are mercenary groups with fully evolved political aims and a focus on financial acquisition and power expansion; they embrace *quasi-terrorism* or true *terrorism* to achieve these goals. Operating in a global context, third generation gangs are true *net warriors* that challenge the legitimacy of state power and institutions. Sullivan (1997) does not qualify any gang as a true third generation gang but concedes that there are organizations that are progressing toward becoming actual third generation gangs (pp. 95–108). In Table 5.1 below, Sullivan elaborates on those concepts regarding gangs in their developmental stages further.

A true third generation gang is essentially an organization for hire that executes political violence on behalf of another party. Manwaring (2005) states that "First and Second Generation Gangs' actions expand their geographical parameters, as well as their commercial and political objectives" (p. 10). This is done in an effort to maintain dominance of a market and increase the market geography that can be saturated by their product. Street and political violence are used to maintain influence over the geographical area over which the cartel presides.

Ultimately, the ability to maintain zones of influence, especially in areas that are poorly governed, or are made ungovernable due to the third generation gang's monopoly of violence within the area, allows for the open movement of the gang and its enterprises. Additionally, the influence that the gang is able to maintain garners political force within their area of operation, creating out of the leader(s) of the gang a warlord or drug baron who exercises a monopoly of violence and influence outside of the traditional state institutions within an already sovereign state. As Manwaring (2005) states, "[T]hat, in turn, takes us back to the relationship between warlordism/drug baronism and insurgency"(p. 10).

Table 5.1. Other Key Concepts/Ideas Discussed by Sullivan (1997) Regarding Gangs in Their Development

Terrorism:	Violence directed at effecting immediate or revolutionary change of political or social forms.
Quasi-terrorism:	Overt violent acts by groups or individuals whose primary goal is extortive or aimed at protecting a criminal enterprise.
Societal warfare:	Embraces both terrorism and quasi-terrorism, more specifically violence aimed at influencing social, political, or economic forms or supporting an organized criminal enterprise which threatens the underlying social fabric or the viability of civil society (i.e., conflict between competing social or cultural values).
Narco-terrorism:	A hybrid of political, social and economic conflict, i.e., a blend of classic terrorism and quasi-terrorism. Perhaps best characterized by the activities of cartels in Colombia, this can be viewed as nascent societal warfare or netwar.
NetWer:	Describes the blurring of crime and war. It is conflict and high intensity crime short of war, i.e., activity currently termed low intensity conflict (LIC), operations other than war (OOTW) and grey area phenomena. Characterized by disruption of information and systems it is exploited by network-based, "internetted" organizations tailored to manipulate information and social perception.
Net Warriors:	Non-state actors organized as networks and engaged in non-regular, societal warfare, i.e., terrorism, and high intensity crime. These actors can be expected to target and exploit information and communications in the future.

Source: Sullivan (1997), p. 98

Latin American Issue

Hal Brands (2009) argues that "Latin America has proven particularly vulnerable to this [third generation gang] phenomenon" as it

has porous borders and numerous illegal markets, and is awash with guns—all factors conducive to organized crime. Corruption is endemic, and state institutions are weak. Widespread poverty and

Table 5.2. Organized Crime Statistics for Latin America and the Caribbean

---

- Forty-three out of the 50 world's most dangerous cities are in Latin America and the Caribbean.
- The 20 most violent cities (according to homicide rate) are in Latin America and the Caribbean with the exception of Cape Town, South Africa.
- Of the 50 urban areas with the highest homicide rates,
    - 16 are in Brazil
    - 9 are in Mexico
    - 6 are in Colombia
    - 6 are in Venezuela
- San Pedro Sula, Honduras, ranked as the most violent city in the world for the 3rd consecutive year, followed by Caracas, Venezuela, and Acapulco, Mexico.

Source: Ortega (2014)

social alienation ensure the gangs a steady supply of young recruits. Densely packed urban slums give them near-impenetrable havens in which to operate. Finally, the deportation of tens of thousands of gang members from the United States over the past 15 years has overwhelmed local law enforcement systems.

Mastering the long-established strategy of *plata o plomo* ("money or bullets") to corrupt officials, these Latin American and Caribbean gangs are successfully undermining already weakened political institutions and further alienating the state from its people (Brands, 2009). The Inter-American Development Bank cites that economic costs of Latin American gang-related violence equates to roughly 14% of the gross domestic product (GDP) (Brands, 2009). Polls show a decline in the region's confidence in democracy, causing analysts to believe that its democracies "are being hollowed out from within" (Brands, 2009). As illustrated by the staggering statistics provided in Table 5.2, public security in Latin America and the Caribbean is eroding, and instability continues to and increasingly threatens the sovereign states in the region.

Importance to the United States

A complex issue with crime and violence of a "transnational nature ... means that no single country can address the issue alone." Brands (2009) further states that "the gang problem is inextricably tied to other problems—such as poverty, corruption, and the structural weakness." Overcoming these increasingly prevalent and powerful gangs will require a multidimensional strategy that will need to include bolstering internal security capabilities, strengthening international and regional cooperative efforts, and implementing and strengthening social programs that address underlying factors aiding gang activity. While Latin America shares a literal border with the United States, the Caribbean has also long been considered a geographical neighbor to the nation—termed the "Third Border" under the Bush Administration in 2001 (The White House, 2001). Security challenges faced by both Latin America and the Caribbean are strongly intertwined with those of the U.S. due, in part, to geopolitical proximity and trade.

The Caribbean islands, several Central American states, and Mexico are considered "well documented" and "major conduit[s]" for the trafficking of people and illicit goods—both in and out of the U.S.—whose profits are "reinforcing terrorist networks" and causing regional instability (McDavid, 2011). Sullivan (2008) notes that Mara Salvatrucha (MS-13) and Eighteenth Street (M-18) originated in Los Angeles and, as a result of voluntary and forced deportation, these gangs have now settled in Latin America, notably Honduras, El Salvador, and Guatemala. MS-13 and M-18 also have "an established presence in Washington, D.C., Maryland, Tennessee, New York City, Houston, and elsewhere in the US." Sullivan asserts that immigration and deportation policy—solidified by *prisonization*—of the U.S., particularly in the City of Los Angeles with MS-13 and M-18, has played an integral role in the evolution (and migration) of gangs. Prisons aid in the development and indoctrination of gang culture; they serve as bases for recruitment and communication, serving as "key node[s]" in a gang's internal network.

IMPLICATIONS

Historically, Louise Shelley (2005) notes that gangs "benefited from the existence of a stable state" (p. 102) in that they successfully exploited the existing political and economic structures in order to further their criminal enterprises. By utilizing corruption and political influence, power—that is, the financial gain of the group—grows relative to the licit flows of the government (Renken, 2013). Due to forces such as globalization and the democratization of technology, however, gangs continue to evolve within the ever-changing political landscape just as individuals and states have to remain relevant actors. Technology connects citizens around the world and, as they may be compelled to group together, has led to an increase in the presence and influence of actors within the world stage (Hammes, 2004, pp. 33–35). This diffusion of power presents an opportunity in which non-state actors can more successfully challenge what used to be a sovereign state monopoly in domestic and world affairs.

While third generation gangs may not exist quite yet, Sullivan (2008) acknowledges that current transnational gangs and criminal organizations are moving into that state of evolution. As individuals, criminal or non-criminal, start to realize the implications of the Internet and globalization, they become empowered. Citizens can use technology to communicate, organize, and ensure their voices are heard on political and social issues such as the "One Million Voices Against the FARC" in Colombia in 2008 (SecDev Foundation & Igarapé Institute, 2013). Contrary to this, transnational gangs and insurgents use these tools to further their activities. They are able to recruit new members, spread their message through international news coverage and propaganda, commit cybercrime, find and track targets, as well as sell their products and services via the Internet (Bjelopera & Finklea, 2012). Second generation gangs are starting to slowly realize they have the tools and capability to lead political movements (insurgencies) in uprooting these existing institutions. They would no longer have to struggle against the established governments; transnational gangs could, in essence, operate and expand freely.

This can be seen in how these organized criminal movements flourish in "lawless zones." While not actually lawless, these mal-governed spaces or areas are those in which the government has lost coercive and political control to these criminal and rebel groups (Sullivan, 2008). The gangs are efficiently organized in a way that makes their groups strong yet "loose" in order to make them "less vulnerable to intrusion" by those trying to dismantle them (Renken, 2013). Gangs and insurgents in these lawless zones utilize violence and coercion on the area's citizens to solidify their presence and claim a monopoly. According to O'Neill (2005), if the people in the area feel they are being neglected by the legitimate government, they may be swayed to support the criminal element if it provides for their basic needs.

This illustrates the truth in Sullivan's (2008) statement that "Law enforcement is constrained by a 'world without borders,' while international criminals operate in a 'borderless' world." Criminal organizations and insurgent movements, as a result, have an advantage in these *asymmetric* and *unconventional* conflicts against states. *Asymmetric warfare* denotes conflict in which the actors are not of equal military capability or strategy such as conflict between a state and armed militant group (Ayalon & Jenkins, 2014, p. 1). Lindsay (1962) describes *unconventional warfare* as conflict in which the involved actors are not all regular armies of sovereign states.

As emerging third generation gangs broaden their *borderless* world through implementation of the technology, and continue their transnational criminal and increasingly political activities, they essentially interact with or eventually become insurgent movements (Manwaring, 2005, p. 10). As these two criminal elements come to perpetuate one another or become one and the same, they become that much more pervasive and dangerous to existing the political institutions and states. Criminal and insurgent organizations gain increasingly more in terms of land occupation, social and political support, and material resources. As a result, it becomes more difficult for counterinsurgent operations and state law enforcement to respond effectively (O'Neill, 2005, pp. 190–191).

CONCLUSION

While many are concerned with the Middle East and its rising threat of spiritual insurgency in the form of ISIS or ISIL, and rightfully so, there should also be a stronger focus on the Latin American struggle against *commercial insurgency*. The former insurgency desires expansion and power to further its political and religious goals in relation to dominance in the region and worldwide effect (Cronin, 2015). The latter arises from a more criminal origin—a desire for increased power and wealth until the third generation gang realizes the stand it can take politically without a recognized state and its institutions. A number of rising examples in Latin America are the various *maras*—current or upcoming Central American third generation gangs such as MS-13 and M-18—as well as *Los Zetas*—a relatively small trafficking and distribution cartel based in Mexico that is increasingly lucrative and seeking relations with various gangs throughout Central America and the U.S. (Brands, 2009).

ISIS has received its desired worldwide recognition of its efforts and mission through highly effective implementation of technology (Talbot, 2015). The success of the gangs and insurgencies in the southern half of the Western Hemisphere is, in part, a result of the same utilization of technology. The "borderless" cyber-world in which they operate to gain land, people, and power has proven extremely difficult for current standards and law enforcement capabilities to combat (O'Neill, 2005, pp. 190–191). Central and South America have always been and seem to be increasingly right in the U.S.'s "own backyard" as technology and growing transnational threats such as evolved gangs and insurgencies are "linked by computers and the Internet" (Taylor, 2004, p. 20).

The groups utilize the "cutting-edge communication technologies and the latest encryption software … [to] establish diverse, secure control and communications centers," to organize massive numbers of disgruntled individuals who identify with the cause or seek the means to uproot existing institutions they do not support (O'Neill, 2005). This global interconnectedness requires action from all state actors involved in or affected by conflict at the hands of these transnational and emerging third generation gangs and insurgent movements. They continue to exploit globalization and technology in order to "gain in sophistication, political interest, and international reach" (Sullivan, 2008). These gangs and insurgent groups are realizing their potential for power within the world stage. States as well as everyday citizens are suffering physically, socially, and economically as a result. The United States, Latin America, and the Caribbean could benefit from, and should participate in, shared efforts to counteract what Renken (2013) considers "one of the most frightening manifestations" of the strongly interconnected and interdependent world of today.

Note: The views expressed in this article are those of the authors and do not necessarily reflect the official policy or position of the Department of the Army, the Department of Defense, or the U.S. Government. This article is cleared for public release; distribution is unlimited.

REFERENCES

Ayalon, A., & Jenkins, B. M. (2014). *War by what means, according to whose rules? The challenge for democracies facing asymmetric conflicts.* Santa Monica, CA: RAND Corporation. Retrieved from www.rand.org/content/dam/rand/pubs/conf_proceedings/CF300/CF334/RAND_CF334.pdf

Bjelopera, J. P., & Finklea, K. M. (2012). Organized crime: An evolving challenge for U.S. law enforcement. *Congressional Research Service Report for Congress.* Retrieved from www.fas.org/sgp/crs/misc/R41547.pdf

Brands, H. (2009). Gangs and the new insurgency in Latin America. *World Politics Review.* Retrieved from www.worldpoliticsreview.com/articles/3882/gangs-and-the-new-insurgency-in-latin-america

Cronin, A. K. (2015). ISIS is not a terrorist group: Why counterterrorism won't stop the latest Jihadist threat. *Foreign Affairs*. Retrieved from www. foreignaffairs.com/articles/middle-east/isis-not-terrorist-group

Department of the Army. (2014). *FM 3-24/MCWP 3-33.5: Insurgencies and countering insurgencies*. Retrieved from http://army-pubs.army.mil/doctrine/DR_pubs/dr_a/pdf/fm3_24.pdf

Hammes, T. X. (2004). *The sling and the stone: On war in the 21st century*. Minneapolis: Zenith Press.

Herd, W. M. (2002). Current unconventional warfare capability versus future war requirements. *U.S. Army War College Strategy Research Project*. Retrieved from www.hit-pages.com/doc/5847494525190144/1

Kilcullen, D. (2010). *Counterinsurgency*. New York: Oxford University Press.

Lindsay, F. A. (1962). Unconventional warfare. *Foreign Affairs*. Retrieved from www. foreignaffairs.com/articles/asia/1962-01-01/unconventional-warfare

Manwaring, M. G. (2005). *Street gangs: The new urban insurgency*. Carlisle, PA: Strategic Studies Institute. Retrieved from www.strategicstudiesinstitute. army.mil/pdffiles/PUB597.pdf

McDavid, H. A. (2011). The Caribbean: The third U.S. border. *FOCALPoint*. Retrieved from www.focal.ca/en/publications/focal point/394-february-2011-hilton-a-mcdavid

Metz, S. (1993). *The future of insurgency*. Carlisle, PA: Strategic Studies Institute. Retrieved from www.strategicstudiesinstitute.army.mil/pdffiles/00333.pdf

O'Neill, B. E. (2005). *Insurgency & terrorism: From revolution to apocalypse*. Washington, DC: Potomac Books.

Ortega, Jose A. (2014). *Por tercer año consecutivo, San Pedro Sula es la ciudad más violenta del mundo* [For the third consecutive year, San Pedro Sula is the world's most violent city]. Mexico City, Mexico: El Consejo Ciudadano para la Seguridad Pública y la Justicia Penal [The Citizen Council for Public Safety and Criminal Justice]. Retrieved from www.seguridadjusticiaypaz.org.mx/sala-de-prensa/941-por-tercer-ano-consecutivo-san-pedro-sula-es-la-ciudad-mas-violenta-del-mundo

Renken, J. (2013). 3rd generation gangs: Criminal insurgents. *Medium. com*. Retrieved from https://medium.com/@5nchange/3rd-genera-tion-gangs-41fddb3a8d71#.5uabftl9g

SecDev Foundation & Igarapé Institute. (2013). *Strategic note: Cyberspace & open empowerment in Latin America.* Retrieved from http://new.secdev-foundation. org/wp-content/uploads/2015/11/OEI-Strategic-Note-25-6-13.pdf

Shelley, L. (2005). The unholy trinity: Transnational crime, corruption, and terrorism. *Brown Journal of World Affairs, 6*(2), 101–111. Retrieved from https:// blackboard.angelo.edu/bbcswebdav/institution/LFA/CSS/Course%20Material/ BOR3304/readings/Shelley%20-%20The%20Unholy%20Trinity.pdf

Sullivan, J. P. (1997). Third generation gangs: Turf, cartel, and net warriors. *Transnational Organized Crime, 3*(3), 95–108. Retrieved from www.academia.edu/1117258/Third_Generation_Street_Gangs_ Turf_Cartels_and_Net_Warriors

Sullivan, J. P. (2008). Transnational gangs: The impact of third generation gangs in Central America. *Air and Space Power Journal.* Retrieved from www.airpower. maxwell.af.mil/apjinternational/apj-s/2008/2tri08/sullivaneng.htm

Talbot, D. (2015). Fighting ISIS online. *MIT Technology Review.* Retrieved from www.technologyreview.com/s/541801/fighting-isis-online

Taylor, P. D. (Ed.). (2004). *Latin American security challenges: A collaborative inquiry from North and South.* Newport, RI: Naval War College Press. Retrieved from www.usnwc.edu/Publications/Naval-War-College-Press/- Newport-Papers/Documents/21-pdf.aspx

U.S. Government. (2012). *Guide to analysis of insurgency.* Retrieved from www. mccdc.marines.mil/Portals/172/Docs/SWCIWID/COIN/Doctrine/ Guide%20to%20the%20Analysis%20of%20Counter insurgency.pdf

The White House. (2001). *Caribbean third border initiative: Fact sheet.* New York: Council on Foreign Relations. Retrieved from www.cfr.org/world/ caribbean-third-border-initiative/p28002

José de Arimatéia da Cruz is a Professor of International Relations/ Comparative Politics at Armstrong State University in Savannah, Georgia, and an Adjunct Research Professor at the U.S. Army War College in Carlisle, Pennsylvania. Dr. da Cruz holds a Bachelor of Arts in Philosophy from Wright State University in Dayton, Ohio; a Master of Arts in Professional Communications and Leadership from Armstrong State University; a Master of Arts in Political Science/Political Philosophy from Miami

University in Oxford, Ohio; a Master of Science in Criminal Justice with an emphasis in Cyber Affairs and Security from Armstrong State University; and a PhD in Political Science from Miami University.

Taylor Alvarez graduated recently with her Bachelor of Arts in Political Science along with minors in Spanish and International Studies. This fall, she will be attending Embry-Riddle Aeronautical University to begin her Master of Science in International Security and Intelligence. Her primary research interest lies in how technology furthers the commission of organized crime and terrorism, particularly in Latin America and the Caribbean.

James Madison Marye is a Senior at Armstrong State University graduating in the Summer of 2016 with a Bachelor of Arts in Political Science. His primary research focus has been on insurgency/counterinsurgency and international relations in South America and the Middle East/North Africa regions. Upon graduation, Marye plans to join the U.S. Army.

Corresponding Author

José de Arimatéia da Cruz
Criminal Justice, Social & Political Science
Armstrong State University
jose.dacruz@armstrong.edu

CPSIA information can be obtained
at www.ICGtesting.com
Printed in the USA
FSHW021716211220
77071FS